Bicyc
Canadia

A Planning Guide and
Stories of Seven Trips

David E. Siskind

Books About Bicycling
Minneapolis, Minnesota

BICYCLING THE CANADIAN ROCKIES
A Planning Guide and Stories of Seven Trips

by David E. Siskind

Published by:
Books About Bicycling
5812 Thomas Circle
Minneapolis, MN 55410-2936
612-929-4498
dsiskind@msn.com

Drawings by Theresa Scanlan, done on her 1986 trip plus a T-shirt design for her sister Elizabeth's 1991 trip.

First Printing April 2002
Printed in the United States of America

ISBN 0-9678878-1-X 12.95

Cover: Tom O'Brien, Jim Nelson, Marv Hondl, and Ed Rapoport
        approaching Beauty Creek in Jasper National Park, 2001.
Inside front cover: Daniel Siskind, age 11, at the Columbia Icefield
        Chalet, Jasper National Park,, 1982.
Inside rear cover: Over Bow Pass and towards Bow Lake and the
        Crowfoot Glacier, 1995.
Rear Cover: Jim Nelson and Marv Hondl on the Icefields Parkway,
        2001

Acknowledgments

First and most, I thank those who have done these trips with me and made them the memorable experiences they have been. That includes my wonderful and adventuresome wives Sylvia and Dana and our children Lisa, Theresa, Daniel, Patrick, and Elizabeth. A very belated thanks to George Colerich of the Minnesota AYH who suggested this trip way back in 1973.

I was most amazed to learn what determined 11 year olds can do, surpassing anything I could have dreamed of when I was that age. The other end of the range are Charley Field, Jacque Lindskoog, and Tom O'Brien who are living proof that you are only as old as you feel.

Thanks to those who read the drafts, provided suggestions and corrected my terrible writing, including Lois O'Brien, Marie Barrett, and Dana.

Finally, thanks to Park Canada who have created and continue to protect this beautiful land, and the Canadian Youth Hostel Association for being such wonderful hosts. I recall with special fondness staying with Olga Forbes at Whiskey Jack, Tony Chatham at Spray River and later Mosquito Creek, and Volker at Maligne Canyon.

Daniel washing dishes at Mosquito Creek

by Theresa Scanlan

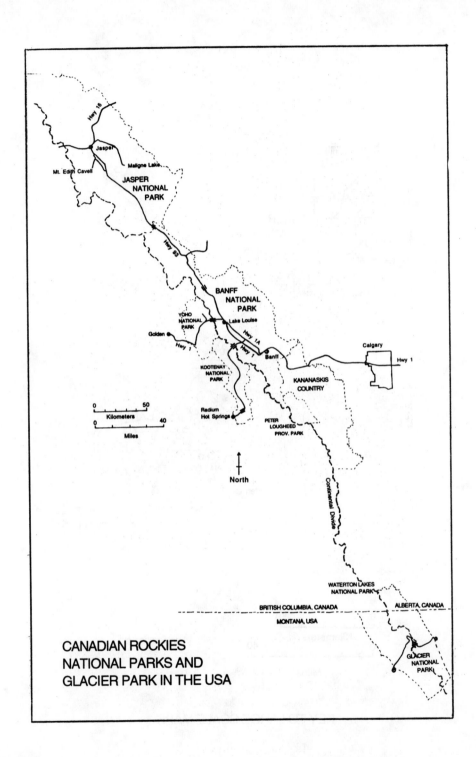

CANADIAN ROCKIES
NATIONAL PARKS AND
GLACIER PARK IN THE USA

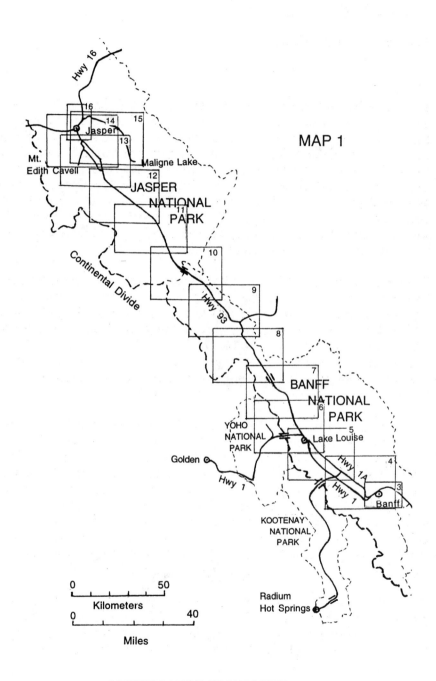

MAP 1

KEY TO LARGE-SCALE MAPS

Chapter 1

The Nature of the Place

The Canadian Rockies National Parks of Banff, Jasper, Yoho and Kooteney are probably the best place for mountain area road biking in the world. The mountains on both sides of the Continental Divide between Alberta and British Columbia rise dramatically out of the forested valleys with no extensive foothills. Views take in up to 2,500 vertical meters of glacier-fed rivers, dense woods of lodgepole pines, aspen and spruce, scree slopes, rocky headwalls and snow fields in the cirques and on mountain tops. When clouds are not pouring over the western ramparts, there is a deep blue sky and air so clear it looks like you could reach out and touch the mountains.

What makes this 20,255 square km mountain preserve great for bike touring is that it is so accessible while being so impressive. Connecting the town sites of Banff to Lake Louise is the 56-km Bow Valley Parkway that was once part of the Trans-Canada Highway. This is old and narrow, winds a bit, is usually not busy, and has a speed limit of 60 km/hr. Most traffic including and especially trucks are on the relocated and newer freeway-like Trans-Canada Highway (National Highway 1) on the other side of the Bow River.

North of Lake Louise is the dramatic 229-km Icefields Parkway to Jasper. This road through deep mountain valleys was originally completed in 1939 and upgraded and paved between 1956 and 1961. So named because it passes the Athabasca Glacier and Columbia Icefield, it is increasingly busy with tourist buses and RV's. Heavy through-truck traffic is banned, however, the road has broad paved shoulders making it safe to bike. In addition to this main route connecting the Towns of Banff and Jasper, there are side trips of similar beauty and challenge, several around the Jasper townsite and especially across the Continental Divide in Yoho Park.

A clarification of names: Banff and Jasper are Canadian national parks on the Alberta side of the Continental Divide. They are also the names of the largest towns in each of those two parks. Lake Louise is both a townsite and a Lake. The town of Lake Louise is in the Bow

Valley where the Trans-Canada Highway, train tracks, and most of the tourist facilities are located. Lake Louise lake is a few miles removed, 200 meters uphill, and has the famous Chateau on its shore.

The parks charge entrance fees but there is a question of their uniformity and if all gate agents know the rules and rates. I believe it to be $5 per day per person or an annual pass good for all the western parks for $35. We were able to obtain a group pass in 2001 for $70, good for 7 persons at all the mountain parks and were told it costs $53 for seniors. Whatever, passes can be purchased at the park gates or in advance from: Superintendent, Banff National Park, P.O. Box 900, Banff, Alberta T0L OCO, Tel. 403-762-1510, Fax. 403-762-1583, www. parkscanada.pch.gc.ca/Banff

Some stats: The town of Banff, resident population 7,716 in the 2000 census, is the highest in Canada at 1,383 meters and Lake Louise, population 1,500, is the highest permanent settlement at 1,536 meters.

Banff Park alone has about 2,500 elk in summer, 2,500 bighorn sheep, 800 mountain goats, 50-80 moose, 850-950 mule deer, 300-350 white-tailed deer, 50-80 grizzlies, 50-60 black bears, 30-40 wolves, 150-250 coyotes, and 4.3 million annual human visitors.

Jasper is a smaller town with about 3,300 residents and is at an elevation of 1,067 m.

The mountain valleys and main highways in Banff and Jasper National Parks run northwest-southeast. For simplicity of notation, Jasper is considered "north" and Banff "south."

Distances are in kilometers and elevations in meters in the text, maps and profiles in this book. Note that one kilometer (km) equals 0.62 miles and one meter (m) equals 3.28 feet.

Wood Stove at Edith Cowell.

Chapter 2

It's Not So Tough

Despite looking rugged and having glacial caps, these mountains are not as lofty as those to the south in the USA. Likewise, the roads and passes are lower and easier. The summits range from 2,700 to 3,400 meters and the highest elevation on the paved roads is 2,068 meters at Bow Pass. The high latitudes (that these mountains are so far north) accounts for the always present snow and cool temperatures. Only Glacier Park in the USA has snow-topped mountains with similar feelings of awesome closeness. Bicycling through these parks is still a challenge, especially Sunwapta Pass at the Columbia Icefield. However the steep parts are relatively short with maximum vertical climbs of about 500 meters. By contrast, Adventure Cycling's Northern Tier route eastbound in the North Cascades in Washington State climbs steeply for 1,400 uninterrupted meters. Their westbound Trans-America Trail enters the mountains west of Pueblo, Colorado by climbing from about 1,200 to over 3,500 meters.

The down side of the Canadian Rockies can be the weather. There can be snow or near-freezing rain anytime, and the high summer touring season is mostly limited to the two months of July and August. Biking in the area around the Columbia Icefield, in particular, can feel like riding in someone's giant freezer. Some roads are still closed in June for ecological reasons and also because the previous winter's avalanche snow has yet to be cleared out. September bike touring is possible but has higher risks for bad weather.

This book is both a guide and a story of seven bike tours in these parks. I first visited Banff, Jasper, and Yoho Parks in 1973, leading a two-week Minnesota American Youth Hostel (AYH) trip of seven men and four women bicyclists. We stayed in hostels, and put in long miles as appropriate for a strong group averaging 31 years of age. However, we had little in the way of planning resources for this first tour: a National Geographic article, the Alberta Provence highway map, and a list of the hostels in the Canadian Hostel handbook. The handbook included information for calculating the distances between them and where food could be obtained. I had prepared an itinerary based on these distances and my feeling for which days would be a challenge. We planned to cook in teams and occasionally splurge in restaurants.

All being city bred, we found the Icefields Parkway particularly exotic, for it was and still is mostly wilderness (although with traffic). Hostels along this road had and still have no electricity or phones and cooking is by wood or bottled gas. In 1982, I led the first tour suitable for well-prepared children and all my tours since then have used these scaled-back distances. My hope is that this book will encourage bike touring in these parks and help in the planning.

The wrong bus at Saskatchewan River Crossing.

Chapter 3

Getting There - This Can be Tough

The first decision is where to start, Banff or Jasper. All seven of my trips started in Banff, visited Jasper and returned to Banff with a side trip to Yoho on the return. My reasons were:

1. Banff is closer to Minneapolis than is Jasper and is, in fact, closer to almost everywhere else.

2. Banff provides an easier warmup to climbing, with both a higher starting elevation, 1,387 rather than 1,058 meters, and a gradual first ascent to Bow Pass from the south.

There used to be a third reason - train service available directly to Banff. This is no longer true, with Canada's Via Rail now going only to Jasper. Biking both ways on the Icefields Parkway gives new views and experiences, and saving exciting Yoho Valley for the return leg helps reduce the anticlimatic effect.

Options for getting to Banff are:

1. Fly into Calgary and take the shuttle or bike the 130 km to Banff.

2. Drive to Banff and park in the free lot across from the Banff hostel.

3. Bike there, as some of us did for the 2001 trip, from Glacier Park in the USA.

For Jasper, all of the above are possible except that air service is less convenient because the closest main airport is in Edmonton. Train service directly to Jasper is also an option from both Vancouver and from eastern Canada.

11

Chapter 4

Accommodations For the Tough and Not-so-Tough

There are accommodations for all tastes. I have stayed in hotels in France and B&B's in England, and have camped my way across the USA. However, for me and for the Canadian Rockies area, where to stay was a no-brainer. My first trip there in 1973 was as a leader of an AYH trip to an area with a chain of closely spaced hostels. It was natural that we would use them and they have remained my choice for the six trips that followed.

Below are accommodations by category, listed from south to north and keyed to the maps in this guide. Only some of the many hotel/motel possibilities in the towns of Banff and Jasper are listed, generally the less expensive ones. Additional and/or current information, such as open season and especially prices, is best obtained from the respective tourist offices or the places themselves.

Kitchen at Whiskey Jack.

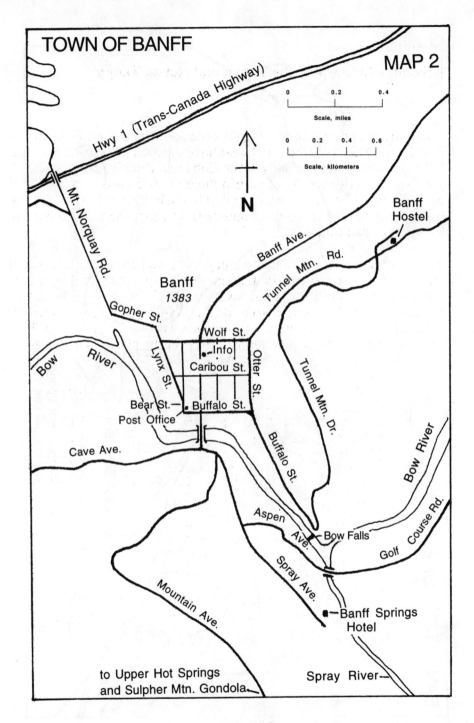

TOWN OF BANFF

MAP 2

Hwy 1 (Trans-Canada Highway)

Scale, miles
0   0.2   0.4

Scale, kilometers
0   0.2   0.4   0.6

N

Banff
Hostel

Mt. Norquay Rd.

Banff Ave.

Tunnel Mtn. Rd.

Banff
1383

Gopher St.

Wolf St.

Bow River

Lynx St.

Info

Caribou St.

Otter St.

Tunnel Mtn. Dr.

Bow River

Bear St.

Buffalo St.

Post Office

Cave Ave.

Buffalo St.

Golf Course Rd.

Aspen Ave.

Bow Falls

Spray Ave.

Mountain Ave.

Banff Springs
Hotel

to Upper Hot Springs
and Sulpher Mtn. Gondola

Spray River

13

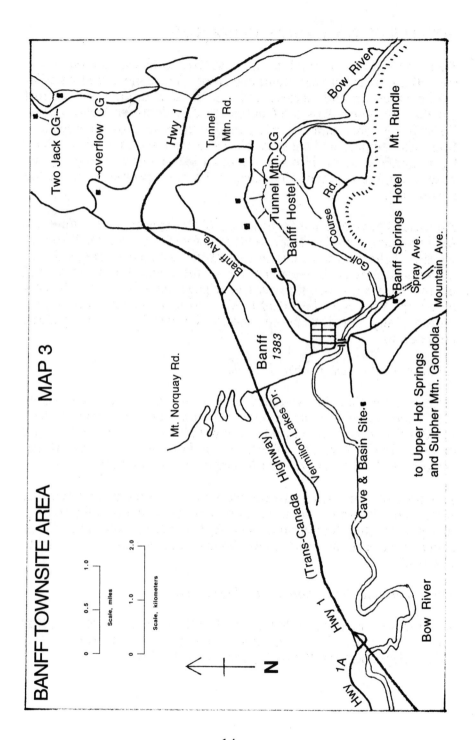

BANFF TOWNSITE AREA   MAP 3

Two Jack CG
overflow CG
Hwy 1
Tunnel Mtn. Rd.
Bow River
Mt. Rundle
Tunnel Mtn. CG
Banff Hostel
Banff Ave.
Course Rd.
Golf
Banff Springs Hotel
Spray Ave.
Mountain Ave.
Banff
1383
Mt. Norquay Rd.
Vermilion Lakes Dr.
(Trans-Canada Highway)
Cave & Basin Site
to Upper Hot Springs
and Sulpher Mtn. Gondola
Bow River
HWY 1
HWY 1A

Scale, miles
0   0.5   1.0

Scale, kilometers
0   1.0   2.0

N

14

HOSTELS OF THE CANADIAN ROCKIES

There are eight Hosteling International (HI) hostels spaced out along the 290-km route between Banff and Jasper. Three more are located in scenic areas around Jasper, and one is at a unique and almost unbelievable site across the Continental Divide in the Yoho Valley. These hostels are quaint, friendly, and inexpensive, provide protection from wild animals, and are great places to meet like-minded travelers. Cost can be a factor. Hostels, although inexpensive, charge by the head. Camping is potentially cheaper if several people share the fee for one site.

All hostels have kitchen facilities usable by guests, and some have food products for sale. Recent additions for cyclists are small roofed weather shelters for the bikes, as long as the rain comes straight down. Many have showers or reasonable facsimiles. Hosteling International membership is not essential but gets trippers better rates, and hostels do accept Visa and MasterCard. With hostels and other accommodations, any specific needs should be verified when making reservations.

Reservation Procedures For Hostels

Hostels in the Canadian Rockies fall into two groups. Those in Banff and Yoho National Parks (Southern Alberta) are administered from the Banff International Hostel in the town of Banff. Those in Jasper National Park (Northern Alberta) are administered from the Jasper International Hostel at Whistler Mountain, close to Jasper.

It is possible for one or two travelers to stay in the hostels without reservations but this is not particularly advised, and especially so for a group. Hostelling International's book, *Hostelling, Experience North America*, says about reservations, "essential for groups and advisable always."

Hostels in Banff Park, Southern Alberta Region

Reservations are obtainable through Banff International Hostel, Box 1358, 801 Coyote Drive (on Tunnel Mountain), Banff, Alberta, T0L 0C0, Telephone: 403-762-4122; Fax: 403-762-3441.

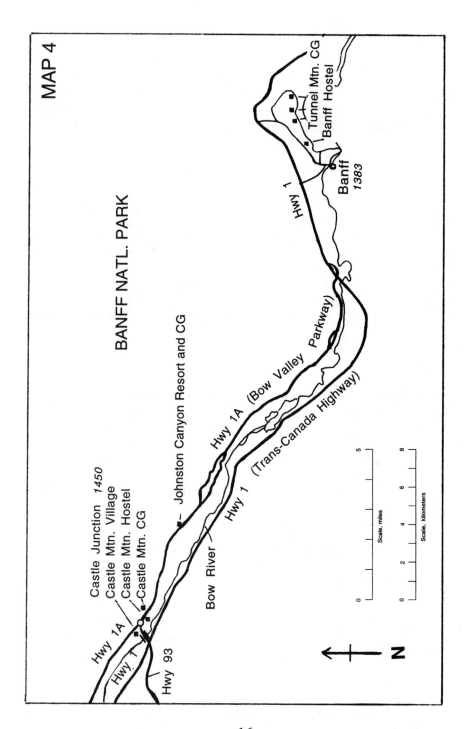

MAP 4

BANFF NATL. PARK

Tunnel Mtn. CG
Banff Hostel
Banff
1383

Hwy 1
Hwy 1

Hwy 1A (Bow Valley Parkway)

Johnston Canyon Resort and CG

Hwy 1 (Trans-Canada Highway)

Castle Junction 1450
Castle Mtn. Village
Castle Mtn. Hostel
Castle Mtn. CG

Bow River

Hwy 1A
Hwy 1
Hwy 93

N

Scale, miles
0   2   4   6   5

Scale, kilometers
0   2   4   6   8

16

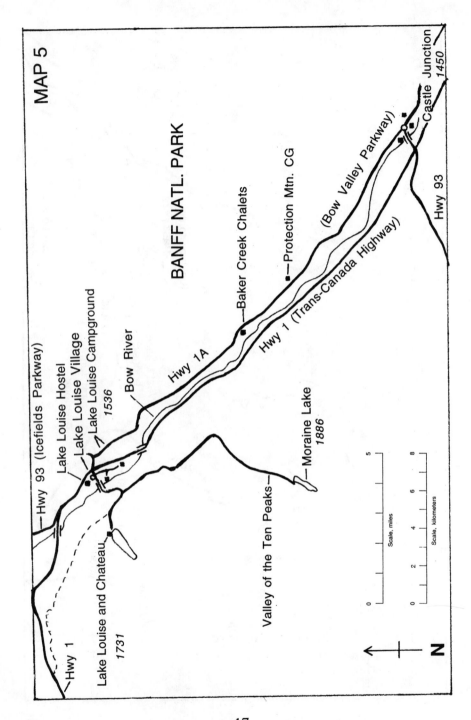

MAP 5

BANFF NATL. PARK

Castle Junction
1450

(Bow Valley Parkway)

Hwy 93

Protection Mtn. CG

Baker Creek Chalets

Hwy 1 (Trans-Canada Highway)

Hwy 1A

Bow River

Hwy 93 (Icefields Parkway)

Lake Louise Hostel
Lake Louise Village
Lake Louise Campground
1536

Moraine Lake
1886

Valley of the Ten Peaks

Hwy 1

Lake Louise and Chateau
1731

Scale, miles
0 2 4 6 5

Scale, kilometers
0 2 4 6 8

N

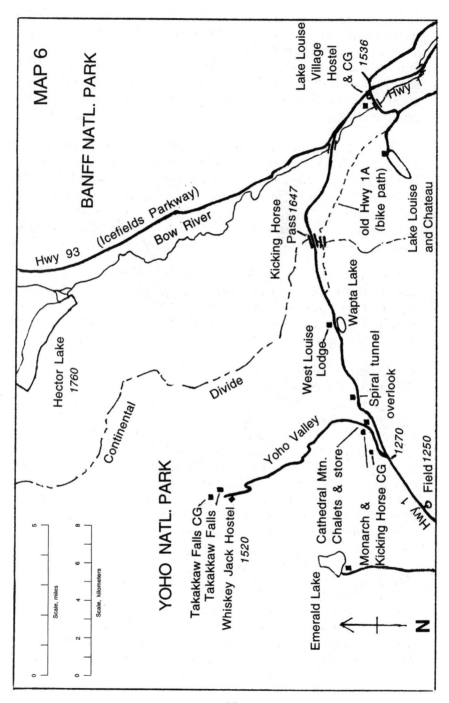

MAP 6

BANFF NATL. PARK

YOHO NATL. PARK

Hwy 93 (Icefields Parkway)

Bow River

Hector Lake 1760

Continental

Divide

Kicking Horse Pass 1647

Lake Louise Village Hostel & CG

1536

Hwy 1

old Hwy 1A (bike path)

Lake Louise and Chateau

Wapta Lake

West Louise Lodge

Spiral tunnel overlook

1270

Field 1250

Hwy 1

Yoho Valley

Takakkaw Falls CG
Takakkaw Falls
Whiskey Jack Hostel
1520

Emerald Lake

Cathedral Mtn. Chalets & store

Monarch & Kicking Horse CG

N

Scale, miles
0   2   4   6   5

Scale, kilometers
0   8   6   4

18

1. Banff International Hostel (Maps 2, 3 and 4). About three km from downtown, northeast up Otter St./Tunnel Mountain Road and considerably uphill. This is a modern hostel with showers, laundry facilities and in-house Cafe Alpenglow. Other amenities are available downtown. The view towards Mt. Rundle is fantastic and makes the front of the hostel a good place to take the first group picture.

2. Castle Mountain Hostel (Map 4). At Castle Junction, Highways 1A and 93. This modernized cabin-type hostel is 33 km north of Banff. The original structure, as with most of the hostels, dates from World War II. Groceries are available across the road, and the closest restaurant is at Johnston Canyon, 6 km south towards Banff. Castle Mountain and Eisenhower Peak with it's meadow "golf course," dominate the view towards the north.

3. Lake Louise Hostel (Maps 5 and 6). In Lake Louise Village just north of the Sampson Mall shopping center, 60 km from Banff. This modern large hostel has a highly-rated cafe and laundry facilities. Other amenities are just a short walk or bike ride to the Mall and village center.

4. Mosquito Creek Hostel (Map 7). On the Icefields Parkway (Highway 93), 84 km north of Banff and 26 km north of Lake Louise Village. This series of simple cabins resembles a small village. The sauna is a work of art as is the dammed-up channel of Mosquito Creek available for cooling down. In this hostel, as with all the simple ones, warmth when needed is provided by wood-burning stoves. There are many food products for sale, or food can be carried from Lake Louise, if going north. The name is puzzling as mosquitos do not seem to be any more concentrated here than elsewhere. A trail goes down to the Bow River with views of the towering peaks to the west.

5. Rampart Creek Hostel (Map 9). On the Icefields Parkway (Highway 93), 11 km north of the Saskatchewan River Crossing and 148 km from Banff. This hostel consists of four simple cabins at the base of a cliff, which is fun for scrambling. Food here can be a problem, as the Crossing no longer sells groceries. It does have a pricey cafeteria and, out back in the Crossing hotel, a decent and reasonably priced restaurant called the Pub.

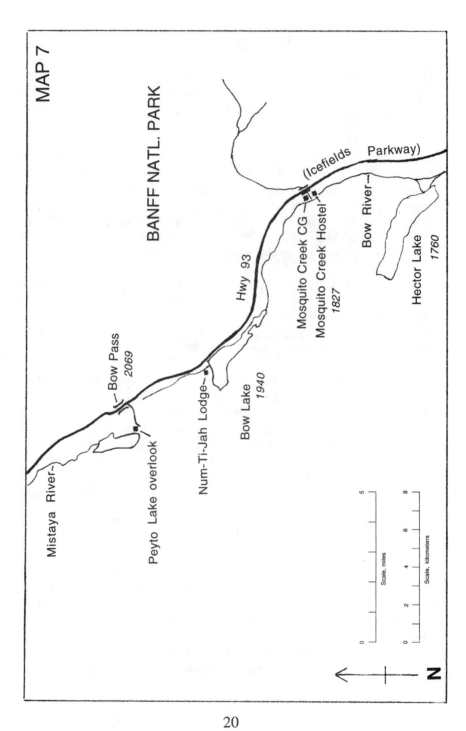

MAP 7

BANFF NATL. PARK

(Icefields   Parkway)

Mosquito Creek CG
Mosquito Creek Hostel
1827

Bow River--

Hector Lake
1760

Hwy 93

Bow Pass
2069

Num-Ti-Jah Lodge--

Bow Lake
1940

Mistaya River--

Peyto Lake overlook

5

8

Scale, miles

Scale, kilometers

6

4

2

0

0

N

20

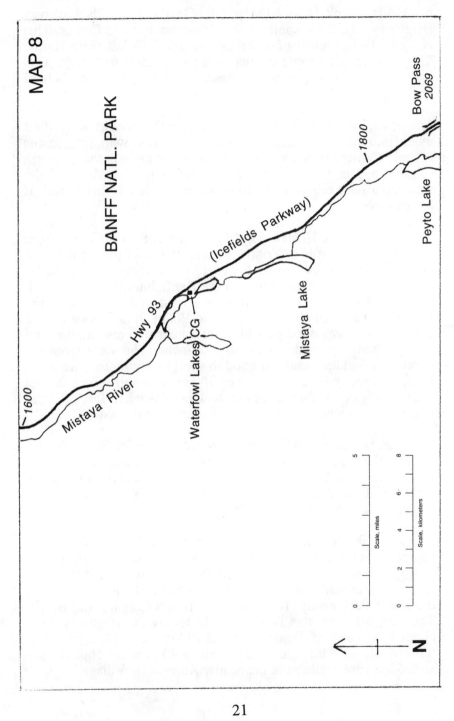

MAP 8

BANFF NATL. PARK

1600

Mistaya River

Hwy 93

(Icefields Parkway)

Waterfowl Lakes CG

Mistaya Lake

1800

Peyto Lake

Bow Pass
2069

Scale, miles

0 2 4 6 8

Scale, kilometers

0 2 4 6

5

N

21

6. Hilda Creek Hostel (Map 10). On the Icefields Parkway (Highway 93), 8 km south of the Columbia Icefield Center. This is also 118 km north of Lake Louise and 178 km from Banff. This is a line of simple cabins, similar to Rampart Creek. This high elevation hostel has a nice alpine meadow a short hike behind and a little uphill.

The hostel does stock some food items but this should be verified when making reservations. No groceries are available at the Icefield Center but you can get pricey meals there at the cafeteria (before 6 p.m.) and restaurant (after 6 p.m.). Most of the Sunwapta pass climbing is done when you reach this hostel, if heading north.

7. Whiskey Jack Hostel (Map 6). This hostel is different from the others in that it is in Yoho National Park over the Continental Divide in British Columbia. However, it is administered by the HI Southern Alberta region through the Banff International Hostel. Whiskey Jack Hostel is about 35 km west of Lake Louise, the final 13 km a tough climb up the Yoho Valley. It is a modern style building that was once part of a hotel near its present site. The hotel is gone - wiped out by an avalanche. The view from the porch is too unique and too good to spoil by trying to describe it here. I hope you can discover it for yourself. This hostel traditionally opens for the season the second week in July after the winter's avalanche snow has been cleared from the road.

Food can be purchased in a store/cafe in the town of Field, about 3 km past the Yoho Valley turnoff. There is also a more convenient but smaller store/cafe after the Yoho Valley turnoff from Highway 1 at the Cathedral Mountain Chalets, across the Yoho River bridge and and just before the steep part of the Yoho Valley climb.

8. Kananaskis Country Hostel (map, inside front cover). This hostel is also different in that it is not in the National Parks but nearby in the less developed Kananaskis Country, SE of Banff. It is also administered by the Southern Alberta Region along with the Banff Park group. It is located between Calgary and Banff. The turn off from the Trans-Canada Highway (Highway 1) is about 46 km east of Banff town and 79 km west of Calgary. The hostel is then 25 km south on Highway 40 near the Nakiska ski area. Meals are available at the nearby Kananaskis Village.

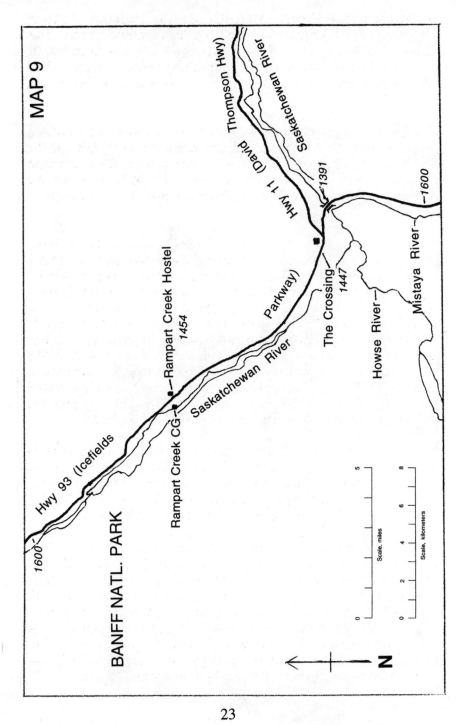

MAP 9

BANFF NATL. PARK

Hwy 93 (Icefields
1600

Rampart Creek Hostel
1454

Rampart Creek CG

Saskatchewan River

Parkway)

The Crossing
1447

Thompson Hwy)

Hwy 11 (David

Saskatchewan River
1391

Howse River

Mistaya River
1600

Scale, miles
0   2   4   6   8
Scale, kilometers

N

23

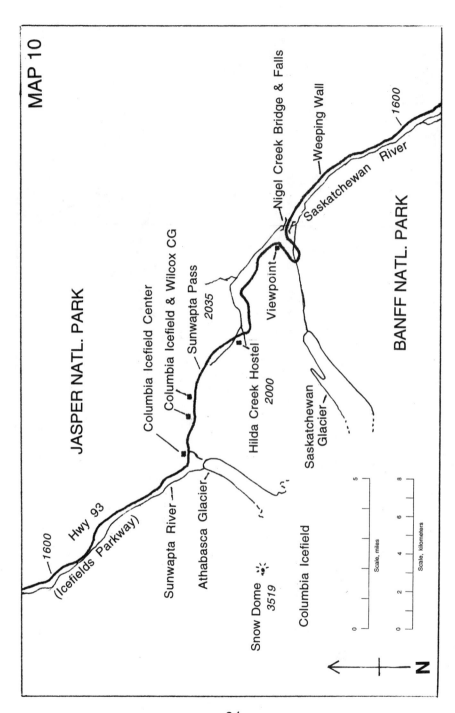

MAP 10

JASPER NATL. PARK

BANFF NATL. PARK

Hwy 93
(Icefields Parkway)
1600

Snow Dome
3519

Columbia Icefield

Sunwapta River

Athabasca Glacier

Columbia Icefield Center

Columbia Icefield & Wilcox CG

Sunwapta Pass
2035

Hilda Creek Hostel
2000

Saskatchewan
Glacier

Nigel Creek Bridge & Falls

Weeping Wall

Viewpoint

Saskatchewan River

1600

Scale, miles

Scale, kilometers

N

24

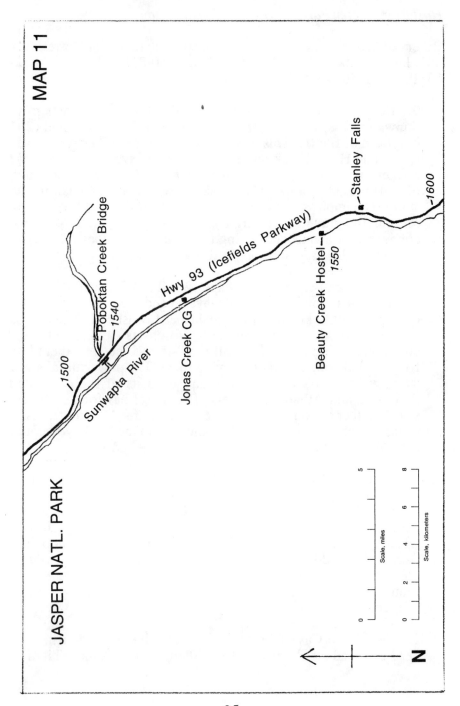

MAP 11

JASPER NATL. PARK

Poboktan Creek Bridge
1540

1500

Sunwapta River

Hwy 93 (Icefields Parkway)

Jonas Creek CG

Beauty Creek Hostel
1550

Stanley Falls

1600

Scale, miles
0   2   4   6   8
Scale, kilometers

N

25

Reservations are obtainable through Jasper International Hostel, Box 387, Jasper, Alberta, T0E 1E0, Telephone: 780-852-3215 or 877-852-0781; E-mail: jihostel@hostellingintl.ca

9. Beauty Creek Hostel (Map 11). North of and down from Sunwapta pass, 17 km north of the Columbia Icefield Center (204 km north of Banff). This is a series of cabins similar to Rampart Creek and Hilda Creek hostels. A shower is available with some bucket handling. The hostel manager stocks food for sale and offered (in 2001) a pancake breakfast with real Canadian maple syrup. The impressive view towards Tangle Ridge and Mt. Wilcox remind the traveler of mighty Sunwapta Pass that was just conquered or awaits addressing the next day, as does the nearby gurgling and cloudy Sunwapta River.

10. Athabasca Falls Hostel (Maps 12 and 13). Located just south of the southern junction of Highways 93 and 93A, 258 km north of Banff and 32 km south of the Jasper townsite. This hostel is four enlarged cabins one of which is a kitchen and common/reading room. Like all the "simple" hostels, there is a friendly and cozy feeling to staying there. The powerful falls is a short walk across the highway and consists of the combined Sunwapta and Athabasca Rivers. The hostel has food items for sale. Another option is to purchase and carry food 24 km from the restaurant at Sunwapta Falls. If coming from the north, you could carry food from Jasper.

11. Maligne Canyon Hostel (Maps 14, 15 and 16). Located 11 km east of Jasper on the Maligne Lake Road, the last 4 km being a pretty steep climb of about 120 m. Getting to Maligne Canyon from the Athabasca Falls Hostel involves going through Jasper, which provides opportunities for laundry, showers, and shopping. Across the road from the hostel is a teahouse where meals can be obtained and also the beginning of the canyon hike. The 80-km roundtrip ride to Maligne Lake and tourist center is a good day ride from the hostel.

12. Mt. Edith Cavell Hostel (Map 13). This is a side trip up a dead-end road off Highway 93A. Although it takes quite a bit of

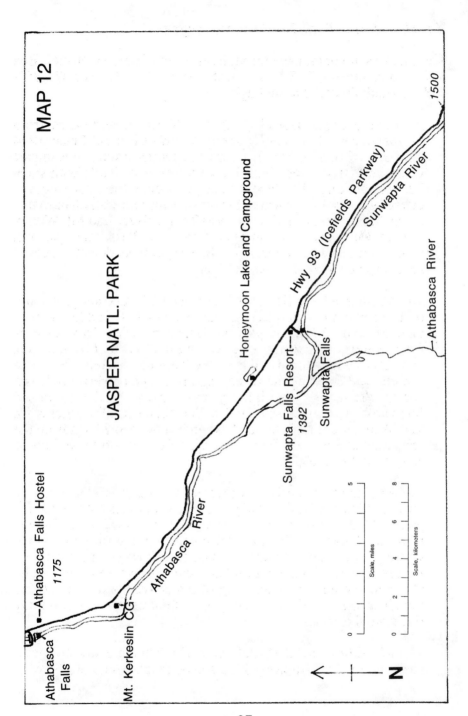

MAP 12

JASPER NATL. PARK

Athabasca Falls Hostel
1175

Athabasca
Falls

Mt. Kerkeslin CG

Athabasca River

Honeymoon Lake and Campground

Hwy 93 (Icefields Parkway)

Sunwapta River

Sunwapta Falls Resort
1392

Sunwapta Falls

Athabasca River

1500

Scale, miles
0   2   4   6   8

Scale, kilometers
0   2   4   6   8

N

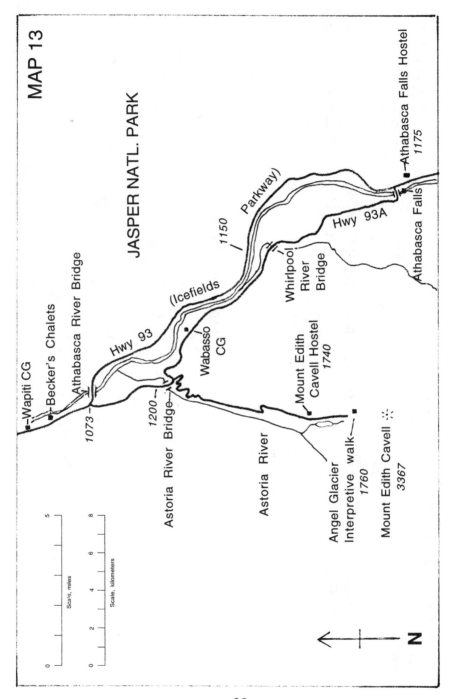

MAP 13

JASPER NATL. PARK

Wapiti CG

Becker's Chalets

Athabasca River Bridge

Hwy 93

1073

1200

Astoria River Bridge

Astoria River

Astoria River

(Icefields

Parkway)

1150

Wabasso CG

Whirlpool River Bridge

Hwy 93A

Mount Edith Cavell Hostel
1740

Angel Glacier Interpretive walk
1760

Mount Edith Cavell
3367

Athabasca Falls Hostel
1175

Athabasca Falls

Scale, miles

Scale, kilometers

N

28

effort to get there, everyone who does it says it is definitely worth it. It is 23 km from Jasper, the last 13 of which are up a narrow switchbacked road, paved but rough in spots. The total climb from Jasper is about 1,400 m. The hostel is similar to to the one at Athabasca Falls - four enlarged cabins with a friendly and cozy atmosphere. The setting is in a narrow valley with imposing close-by rock walls and slopes and a view of dominating snow-covered Mt. Edith Cavell. Within walking distance at the end of the road, about 2 km, is an interpretative hike, Path of the Glacier right under the towering rock wall of Mt. Edith Cavell.

13. Jasper International Hostel (Maps 14 and 16). Located 7 km southwest of the town of Jasper on the Whistler Mountain Road, 0.5 km short of the parking lot for the Skytram lift. This modern large hostel is on the pattern of the International Hostel in Banff. It is newer than the three other Jasper- area hostels, none of my seven trips since 1973 have stayed there. One tripper who had vivited in 2001 described it as less intimate and friendly than the smaller and simpler hostels. It does, however, offer additional services like a coin laundry.

Summarizing the chain of hostels from south to north (actually southeast to northwest):

Hostel	km from last hostel	km from Banff town
Banff Intnl.	- -	3
Castle Mountain	33	33
Lake Louise Intnl.	27	60
Mosquito Creek	26	84
Rampart Creek	64	148
Hilda Creek	30	178
Beauty Creek	26	204
Athabasca Falls	54	258
Maligne Canyon	43	300

The route from Athabasca Falls to Maligne Canyon passes through Jasper. Other options around the town of Jasper are Jasper International and Mt. Edith Cavell. Both of these are south of the Jasper townsite.

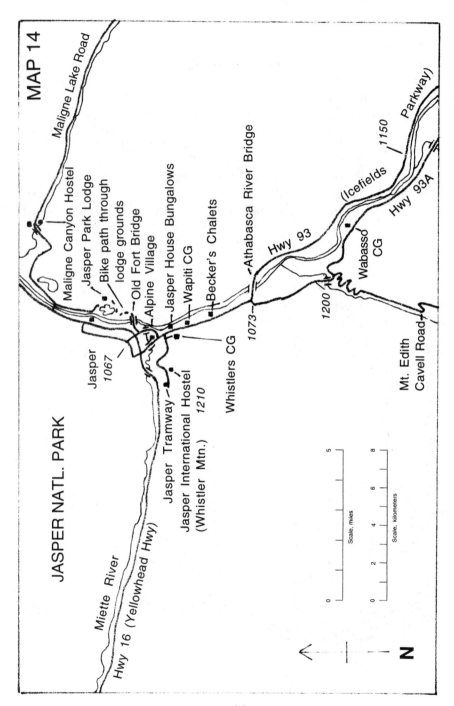

MAP 14

Maligne Lake Road

JASPER NATL. PARK

Maligne Canyon Hostel
Jasper Park Lodge
Bike path through
lodge grounds
Old Fort Bridge
Alpine Village
Jasper House Bungalows
Wapiti CG
Becker's Chalets
Athabasca River Bridge

Jasper
1067

Jasper Tramway
Jasper International Hostel
(Whistler Mtn.)
1210

Whistlers CG

Hwy 93

1073

1200

Wabasso
CG

(Icefields
1150
Parkway)

Hwy 93A

Mt. Edith
Cavell Road

Miette River

Hwy 16 (Yellowhead Hwy)

Scale, miles
0   2   4   6   8
Scale, kilometers
0   5

N

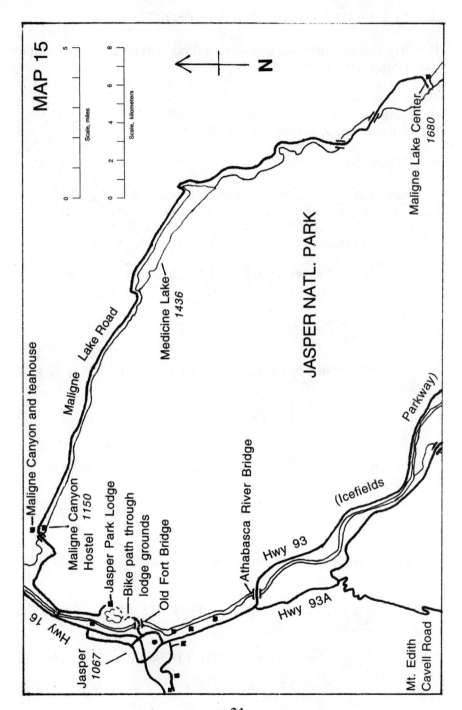

MAP 15

N

Scale, miles

Scale, kilometers

Maligne Canyon and teahouse

Maligne Lake Road

Medicine Lake
1436

JASPER NATL. PARK

Maligne Lake Center
1680

Hwy 16

Jasper
1067

Maligne Canyon
Hostel 1150

Jasper Park Lodge

Bike path through
lodge grounds

Old Fort Bridge

Athabasca River Bridge

Hwy 93

Hwy 93A

(Icefields

Parkway)

Mt. Edith
Cavell Road

31

HOTELS, MOTELS, CABINS AND RESORTS

This trip can be done using resorts and hotel-type accommodations. Not having used them, I cannot personally verify how friendly and pleasant they are or if something special about the trip and the experience will be lost by the privacy (and isolation) they provide. There are quite a few in the towns of Banff, Lake Louise and Jasper but relatively few along the road in between.

Banff Town (Maps 2-4).

There are many choices for accommodations in this, the largest town in these four parks. Some of the less expensive ones (on a relative scale) are listed below. All are in Banff, Alberta T0L 0C0. (A notable example of a pricey place not listed is the Banff Springs Hotel.)

1. The Banff Center, P.O. Box 1020, St. Julien Road and Tunnel Mountain Drive, Tel. 403-762-6308

2. Banff Voyager Inn, P.O. Box 1540, 555 Banff Avenue, Tel. 403-762-3301

3. Banff Y Mountain Lodge, P.O. Box 520, 102 Spray Avenue, Tel. 403-762-3560

4. Driftwood Inn, P.O. Box 1840, 337 Banff Avenue, Tel. 403-762-2207

5. Elkhorn Lodge, P.O. Box 352, 124 Spray Avenue, Tel. 403-762-2299

6. High Country Inn, P.O. Box 700, 419 Banff Avenue, Tel. 403-762-2236

7. Homestead Inn, P.O. Box 669, 217 Lynx Street, Tel. 403-762-4471

8. Irwin's Motor Inn, P.O. Box 1198, 429 Banff Avenue, Tel. 403-762-4566

9. Red Carpet Inn, P.O. Box 1800, 138 Banff Avenue, Tel. 403-762-4184

10. Spruce Grove Motel, P.O. Box 471, 545 Banff Avenue, Tel. 403-762-2112

11. Woodland Village, P.O. Box 398, 449 Banff Avenue, Tel. 403-762-5521

Note that #3, 5 and 10 were listed as having high season (summer) rates of less that $100 in 2001.

Information on additional places, including B&B's, can be obtained from Banff/Lake Louise Tourism Bureau, P. O. Box 1298, Banff, Alberta T0L 0C0, Tel. 403-762-8421. Information is also available from the Banff Visitor Center, Tel. 403-762-1550 and Lake Louise Visitor Center, Tel. 403-522-3833.

Between Banff and Lake Louise (Maps 4-5)

1. Johnston Canyon Resort (Map 4). Located 27 km north of Banff on the Bow Valley Parkway, Highway 1A. Box 875, Banff, Alberta T0L 0C0 Tel. 403-707-2971. There is a restaurant there also.

2. Castle Mountain Village (Map 4). At the junction of Highways 93 and 1A, 33 km north of Banff. Box 1655, Banff, Alberta T0L 0C0 Tel. 403-762-3868. Store & groceries, but no restaurant.

3. Baker Creek Chalets (Map 5). On Highway 1A, 48 km north of Banff and 12 km south of Lake Louise Village. Box 66, Lake Louise, Alberta T0L 1E0, Tel. 403-522-3761. Restaurant. (Note: listed as over $200 per night in 2001.)

Lake Louise Village Area and the road up to the lake (Map 5)

A few less expensive accommodations are listed below. All use the postal address: Lake Louise, Alberta T0L 1E0.

1. Deer Lodge, P.O. Box 100, 109 Lake Louise Drive, Tel. 403-522-3747

2. Lake Louise Inn, P.O. Box 209, 210 Village Road, Tel. 403-522-3791

3. Mountaineer Lodge, P.O. Box 150, 101 Village Road, Tel. 403-522-3844

4. Paradise Lodge and Bungalows, P.O. Box 7, 105 Lake Louise Drive, Tel. 403-522-3595

5. Post Hotel, P.O. Box 69, 200 Pipestone Road, Tel. 403-522-3989

Icefields Parkway, Lake Louise to Athabasca Falls (Maps 7- 12)

1. Simpson's Num-Ti Jah Lodge (Map 7). Located just off the Icefields Parkway (Highway 93) on the north shore of Bow Lake, 39 km north of Lake Louise. Box 39, Lake Louise, Alberta T0L 1E0, Tel. 403-522-2167

2. The Crossing (Map 9). At the junction of Highways 93 and 11, two km north of the Icefields Parkway bridge across the Saskatchewan River or 79 km north of Lake Louise. Bag service 333, Lake Louise, Alberta T0L 1E0, Tel. 403-761-7000. Store and cafeteria are next to the highway and behind is the hotel and restaurant, the Pub.

3. Columbia Icefields Chalet (Map 10). At the Athabasca Glacier, 129 km north of Lake Louise. P.O. Box 1140, Banff, Alberta T0L 0C0, Tel. 780-852-6550, 1-877-423-7433. There is a cafeteria open until 6 p.m. and a restaurant after 6 p.m., both pricey.

4. Sunwapta Falls Resort (Map 12). On the Icefields Parkway (Highway 93) at the turnoff to Sunwapta Falls, 177 km north of Lake Louise and 55 km south of Jasper. Box 97, Jasper, Alberta TE0 1E0, Tel. 780-852-4852, 1-888-828-5777. Has one of the better restaurants and shops along the highways between Banff and Jasper.

Jasper Vicinity (Maps 14 and 16)

1. Alpine Village (Maps 14 and 16). Located 2.5 km south of Jasper on Highway 93A. Box 610, Jasper, Alberta T0E 1E0, Tel. 780-852-3285

2. Becker's (Roaring River) Chalets (Maps 14 and 16). Located 7 km south of Jasper on Highway 93. Box 579, Jasper, Alberta T0E 1E0, Tel. 780-852-3779

3. Jasper House Bungalows (Maps 14 and 16). Located 3.5 km south of Jasper on Highway 93. Box 817, Jasper, Alberta T0E 1E0, Tel. 780-852-4535

4. Patricia Lake Bungalows (Map 16). Located 4.8 km northwest of the Jasper town center on Pyramid Lake Road. Box 657, Jasper, Alberta T0E 1E0, Tel. 780-852-3560

5. Pine Bungalows (Maps 16 and 17). 2 km east of Jasper Townsite on Athabasca River. Box 7, Jasper, Alberta T0E 1E0, Tel. 780- 852-3491

6. Pocahontas Bungalows. Located 43 km east of Jasper off Highway 16 at the Miette Hot Springs Road. Box 820, Jasper, Alberta T0E 1E0, Tel. 780-866-3732, 1-800-843-3372

7. Tekarra Lodge (Map 16). Located 1 km south of Jasper on Miette and Athabasca Rivers. Box 669, Jasper, Alberta T0E 1E0, Tel. 780-852-3058, 1-888-404-4540

Jasper Town (Maps 16 and 17)

Jasper is a smaller town than Banff but still has a variety of accommodation options. Some are listed below, and additional ones are available from Jasper Tourism at 780-852-3858. All have postal addresses: Jasper, Alberta T0E 1E0.

1. Amethyst Lodge, P.O. Box 1200, 200 Connaught Drive, Tel. 780-852-3394, 1-888-8JASPER.

2. Astoria Hotel, P.O. Box 1710, 404 Connaught Drive, Tel. 780-852-3351, 1-800-661-7343.

3. Athabasca hotel, P.O. Box 1420, 510 Patricia St. Tel. 780-852-3385, 1-87SKIATHAB.

4. Bear Hill Lodge, P.O. Box 700, 100 Bonhomme Street, Tel. 780-852-3209

5. Lobstick Lodge, P.O. Box 1200, 94 Geikie Street, Tel. 780-852-4431, 1-888-8JASPER.

6. Maligne Lodge, P.O. Box 757, 930 Connaught Drive, Tel. 780-852-3143, 1-800-661-1315.

7. Marmot Lodge, P.O. Box 1200, 86 Connaught Drive, Tel. 780-852-4471, 1-888-8JASPER.

8. Mount Robson Inn, P.O. Box 88, 902 Connaught Drive, Tel. 780-852-3143, 1-800-587-3327.

9. Tonquin Inn, P.O. Box 658, 100 Juniper Street, Tel. 780-852-4987, 1-800-661-1315.

10. Whistler's Inn, P.O. Box 250, 105 Miette Avenue, Tel. 780-852-3361, 1-800-282-9919.

West of Lake Louise and Yoho Park Area (Map 6)

1. West Lake Louise Lodge. Located on Highway 1, Trans-Canada Highway, 4 km west of Kicking Horse Pass and across the road from Wapta Lake. Box 9, Lake Louise, Alberta T0L 1E0, Tel. 604-343-6311. Also has a decent and reasonable restaurant.

2. Cathedral Mountain Chalets. Located on the Yoho Valley Road, 2 km north of Highway 1, Trans-Canada Highway. Box 9, Field, British Columbia V0A 1G0, Tel. 604-343-6442. Has a store with groceries and also a cafe.

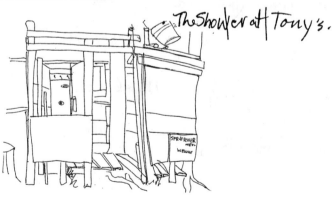

The Shower at Tony's.

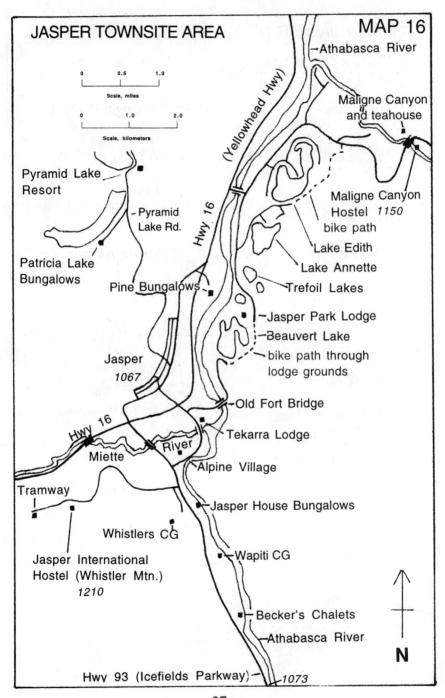

Athabasca River

Maligne Canyon and teahouse

(Yellowhead Hwy)

Scale, miles
0   0.5   1.0

Scale, kilometers
0   1.0   2.0

Pyramid Lake Resort

Pyramid Lake Rd.

Hwy 16

Maligne Canyon Hostel 1150
bike path

Lake Edith

Patricia Lake Bungalows

Lake Annette

Pine Bungalows

Trefoil Lakes

Jasper Park Lodge

Beauvert Lake

bike path through lodge grounds

Jasper 1067

Old Fort Bridge

Hwy 16

Tekarra Lodge

Miette

River

Alpine Village

Tramway

Jasper House Bungalows

Whistlers CG

Wapiti CG

Jasper International Hostel (Whistler Mtn.) 1210

Becker's Chalets

Athabasca River

N

Hwy 93 (Icefields Parkway) 1073

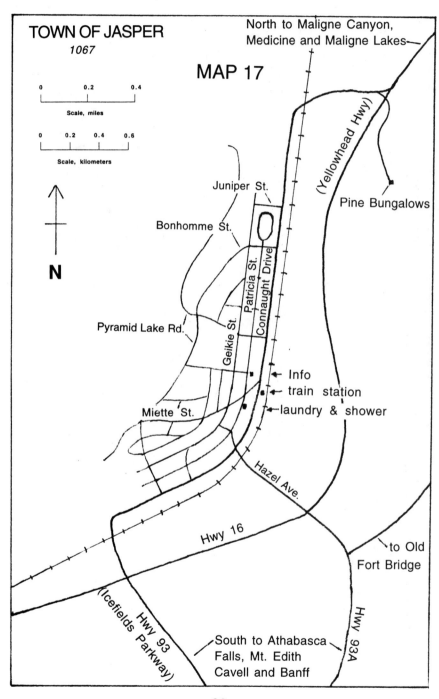

TOWN OF JASPER
1067

MAP 17

North to Maligne Canyon,
Medicine and Maligne Lakes

0   0.2   0.4
Scale, miles

0   0.2   0.4   0.6
Scale, kilometers

N

Juniper St.

Bonhomme St.

Patricia St.

Connaught Drive

(Yellowhead Hwy)

Pine Bungalows

Pyramid Lake Rd.

Geikie St.

Info
train station
laundry & shower

Miette St.

Hazel Ave.

Hwy 16

Hwy 93
(Icefields Parkway)

Hwy 93A

to Old
Fort Bridge

South to Athabasca
Falls, Mt. Edith
Cavell and Banff

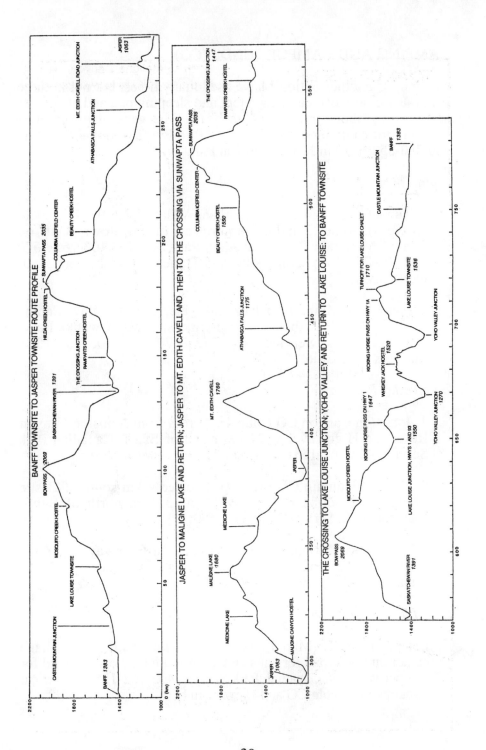

39

CAMPING AND CAMPGROUNDS (CG)

Camping is another option I have used many times, but not in these parks. It would mean carrying a tent and sleeping pad and also incur some worry about intimacy with bears. The general information numbers for camping are 403-762-1550 in Banff National Park and and 780-852-6176 in Jasper National Park.

Banff Town

1. Tunnel Mountain Trailer Court and Village I and II
(Map 3). About 2 and 4 km northeast of downtown Banff on Tunnel Mountain Road. Canadian Park Service, 403-762-1570 and 403-762-1571. Full hookups in Trailer Court, showers in all, electricity in II.

2. Two Jack Main, Two Jack Lakeside, and Overflow Campgrounds (Map 3). About 10 km northeast at Minnewanka Lake. Canadian Park Service, 403-762-1570 and 403-762-1571. Showers in Lakeside.

Bow Valley Parkway

1. Johnston Canyon CG (Map 4). Across from Johnston Canyon Resort on Highway 1A, 27 km north of Banff. Canadian Park Service, 403-762-1581. Showers.

2. Castle Mountain CG (Map 4). Located 1 km south of Castle Mountain Junction on Highway 1A, 32 km north of Banff. Canadian Park Service, 403-762-1550.

3. Protection Mountain CG (Map 5). On Highway 1A, 7 km north of Castle Mountain Junction and also 40 km north of Banff. Canadian Park Service, 403-762-1550.

Lake Louise Area

Lake Louise CG (Map 5). Two areas: 1 km south of the village center on town road for tents and 2 km south on the same road for camper vehicles. Canadian Park Service, 403-762-1550. Electrical hookups in vehicle CG and showers in both.

Icefields Parkway

1. Mosquito Creek CG (Map 7). Across the creek from the hostel, 26 km north of Lake Louise and 86 km north of Banff. Canadian Park Service, 403-762-1550.

2. Waterfowl Lakes CG (Map 8). Located 59 km north of Lake Louise and 119 km north of Banff. Canadian Park Service, 403-762-1550.

3. Rampart Creek CG (Map 9). Across the Parkway from the hostel, 11 km north of the Crossing. This is 90 km north of Lake Louise and 150 km north of Banff. Canadian Park Service, 403-762-1550.

4. Columbia Icefield and Wilcox Campgrounds (Map 10). Located about 2 and 3 km south of the Columbia Icefield Center, or about 124 km north of Lake Louise and 184 km from Banff. Canadian Park Service, 780-852-6176.

5. Jonas Creek CG (Map 11). Located 27 km north of the Columbia Icefield Center, or about 155 km north of Lake Louise and 215 km from Banff. Canadian Park Service, 780-852-6176.

6. Honeymoon Lake CG (Map 12). About 3.5 km north of Sunwapta Falls Resort. This is 181 km north of Lake Louise and 241 km from Banff. Canadian Park Service, 780-852-6176.

7. Mount Kerkeslin CG (Map 12). About 4.5 km south of Athabasca Falls, and 197 km north of Lake Louise and 257 km from Banff. Canadian Park Service, 780-852-6176.

Jasper Town Area

1. Wabasso CG (Maps 13 and 14). On Highway 93A, about 15 km south of the Jasper townsite. Canadian Park Service, 780-852-6176. Electrical hook ups.

2. Wapiti CG (Maps 13, 14 and 16). On Highway 93, about 3 km south of the Jasper. Canadian Park Service, 780-852-6176. Electrical hook ups, showers.

3. Whistlers CG (Maps 14 and 16). South off of Whistler Mountain Road, about 2 km south of Jasper. Canadian Park Service, 780-852-6176. Full hook ups, showers.

4. Marmot Meadows. On Highway 93A south of junction with Highway 93. Group camping only. Canadian Park Service, 780-852-6176.

4. Snaring River CG. Located on Celestine Lake Road off of Highway 16 east of Jasper, 17 km from town center. Canadian Park Service, 780-852-6176. Electrical hook ups

West of Lake Louise and Yoho Park Area (Map 6)

1. Monarch and Kicking Horse Campgrounds. Located near the Cathedral Mountain Chalets on the Yoho Valley Road, 2 km north of Highway 1, the Trans-Canada Highway. Showers in Kicking Horse CG.

2. Takakkaw Falls CG. At the end of the Yoho Valley Road.

The General Store in Yoho.

Chapter 5

Food, Bikes, Packing Lists, and Maps

Nearly anything that can be bought elsewhere can be bought in Banff, Jasper and Lake Louise, for a price. Things tend to be expensive likely because of long distances from everywhere else and possibly because their high season is so short.

FOOD

Information about meals and groceries is included with the discussion of hostels and hotel accommodations in Chapter 4 and in the sample itinerary of Chapter 6.

BIKE SHOPS - bikes and equipment sales and rental

Banff: Bactrax, 225 Bear Street, 403-762-8177
Mountain Magic, 225 Bear Street, 403-762-2591

Lake Louise: Wilson Mountain Sports, Sampson Mall, 403-522-3636

Jasper: Action Gear Cycle, 630 Connaught Drive, 780-852-1111
Freewheel Cycle, 611 Patricia Street, 780-852-3898

Advice on bike equipment is difficult as many people have different styles, experiences, and opinions. What works best is somewhat subjective, for bicycling is both an art and science. My advice is to have a low gear of 30-in or lower (e.g., 28t front x 26t rear on a 27-in wheel or better). This tour is all good pavement so tires can be light touring, although I recommend nothing smaller than 1-1/4 or 700 x 28 mm. Panniers are best for carrying most of the gear and I favor a small handlebar bag for items needed frequently or quickly, such as a camera, sunglasses, and sunscreen. I personally believe that (other than a tandem) if you use both front and rear panniers, you are carrying too much sss-stuff.

43

SAMPLE PACKING LIST - for a two week trip

Documents and the Like:

    Passport or proof of citizenship
    Air and train tickets (if needed)
    Itinerary information
    Tourist info (guide books, maps)
    Money, travelers checks, etc.
    Visa or Master Charge card and PIN
    Hostel Pass (if you plan to use hostels)
    List of important numbers, names and addresses

Clothes:

    Biking shorts (2)
    Long pants for evenings (suitable for riding too if necessary)
    Riding tights for cool mornings
    Biking shirts, short sleeve (4+)
    Biking shirt, long sleeve (1+)
    Bathing suit for sauna (?)
    Underwear, sport tops, sun tops (6)
    Socks (12)
    Windbreaker
    Rain jacket (or rain suit)
    Cold climate: headband or hat, gloves
    Belt, suspenders, etc.
    Gloves (use to call these "track mitts")
    Biking shoes (dual purpose if possible)
    Other shoes (if above cannot be used for walking too)

Personal Items:

    Toiletries (razor, toothbrush, comb, floss...)
    Vitamins and medications
    Soap, shampoo
    Towel
    Suntan lotion/sunscreen
    Laundry detergent (Woolite)
    Sun glasses
    Reading glasses if needed
    Sleeping bag, lightweight

Sports Equipment:

Bike (or arrangements for one)
Helmet
Bags for riding (rear panniers, front panniers or handlebar bag)
Bike computer (optional but handy)
Water bottle
Pump

Tools and Spares:

8, 9,10 mm sockets, 4, 5, 6, mm allen wrenches, spoke wrench
screwdriver set, 6-inch adjustable wrench, chain oil (only one
person need bring all of the above, usually the leader)
Spare brake and shift cables (long, for both front or rear)
Spare tube and patch kit
Spare spokes (to fit wheels plus temporary emergency spokes)
Cable lock and key (a must in all urban areas)
Bungie cords (3)
Small amount of strapping or duct tape

Optional Stuff:

Camera and film (up to 1 roll/day)
Photo filters, extra lenses, etc.
Book (s)
Pen and Paper for trip log,,
 post cards, addresses, etc.
Rubber bands
Plastic bags
Postage stamps
Phone card
Sewing kit

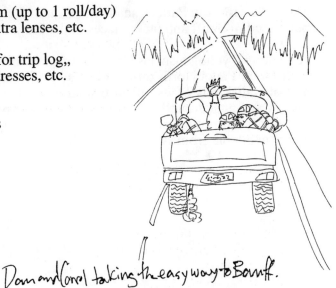

Dan and Carol taking the easy way to Banff.

MAPS

This trip is simple enough that the Alberta Province map provides all the information needed (Travel Alberta, 1-800-661-8888). Also, the maps in this book can be used. For some people, detailed maps add to the adventure of traveling and exploring and several good options exist.

Parks Canada has a pair of maps on 1:200,000 scale, about perfect for cycling. One covers Banff, Yoho, and Kootenay parks and the other Jasper Park. I was able to purchase these at a Minneapolis area map store for about $11 US in 2001.

Gem Trek Publishing has a series of nice "recreational" maps with more cultural detail such as locations and labeling of hostels, campgrounds, and resorts, and shading to help visualize topography. These maps come in varying scales and coverage. The map of the southern part of Banff Park includes Lake Louise and is on a scale of 1:100,000. Five of the Gem Trek maps would be needed to cover the tours in this guide. Some, but not all, were available off-the-shelf in the local map store but it's likely they could be ordered. They were $10 to $11 US each.

The Gem Trek and Parks Canada maps, and likely others, can also be purchased in Banff and other places in the Parks.

Adventure Cycling also has a map of most of this tour as Section 1 of their Great Parks North series. This is specifically a bicyclist's map and has all kinds of useful information on facilities and some on history and background. The route includes the roads between Jasper and Banff but not the side trip to Yoho. The map scale is 1:250,000 and is available from Adventure Cycling Association, Missoula, MT 1-800-721-8719.

Chapter 6

A Sample Itinerary Based on Staying in Hostels

This section describes the route and logistics of a two-week tour of the parks by bicycle. Additional information about the hostels themselves is in Chapter 4 on accommodations.

Day 1 - Banff to Mosquito Creek, 87 km.
Day 2 - Mosquito Creek to Beauty Creek - 120 km
Day 3 - Beauty Creek to Athabasca Falls - 54 km
Day 4 - Athabasca Falls to Maligne Canyon - 43 km
Day 5 - at Maligne Canyon, biking and/or hiking
Day 6 - Maligne Canyon to Mt. Edith Cavell - 34 km
Day 7 - Mt. Edith Cavell to Beauty Creek - 88 km
Day 8 - Beauty Creek to Rampart Creek - 56 km
Day 9 - Rampart Creek to Mosquito Creek - 62 km
Day 10 - Mosquito Creek to Whiskey Jack - 66k
Day 11 - hanging around Whiskey Jack, hiking for sure
Day 12 - Whiskey Jack to Castle Mountain - 62 km
Day 13 - Castle Mountain to Banff - 33 km

The overall logic of this scheme is to get two views of the Parks, coming and going. It also avoids doing two hard passes in one day, provides extra time in places which best warrant it, and a chance to see all the best in the parks. For those who may not have a full 13 days, there are several options. One is to cut out the extra day at Maligne Canyon. Another is to combine short days like 8 and 9 or 12 and 13. This depends on how strong the bikers are. Hilda Creek could be used as a day 7 destination in place of Beauty Creek and Mosquito Creek as day 8, eliminating one overnight. This is not recommended however. Hilda creek is on top of Sunwapta Pass which makes the cold early morning descent less than pleasant.

The schedule listed above provides warm-up periods for all the serious climbs. It is highly recommended that you resist the temptation to skip either Mt. Edith Cavell or Yoho's Whiskey Jack unless the weather is just too bad for the climbs up to them. They are two of the more spectacular areas in the trip.

Long periods of daylight occur this far north in July and a bit less so in August. It is still light at 11 p.m. and, if needed, over 17 hours of riding can be done in daylight. This means it's possible to wait out rain showers, and the days seldom have to be rushed.

DAY-BY-DAY

Afternoon or evening before day 1 - Town of Banff (Maps 2-3)

Downtown Banff has all the amenities such as a post office, restaurants, museums, bike and other shops, supermarket, and a Parks Information office. There are also things worth seeing and experiencing including the Sulpher Mountain Tram, the Banff Springs Hotel, and the hot springs. A nice warmup ride is the Banff Springs Hotel's golf course road. This paved, quiet road loop is about 12 km round trip from downtown and includes dramatic views of Mount Rundal and sometimes wildlife. We encountered a black bear while on an early evening ride there one trip. Banff is very busy in the summer, and many bike tourists will be relieved at leaving town.

Day 1 - Banff to Mosquito Creek via Lake Louise Village, 87 km (Maps 4-7)

Exit Banff via Mt. Norquay Road. Most of the day is spent on the Bow Valley Parkway (Highway 1A) after the first five km on the busy Trans-Canada (Highway 1). There are a few short steep climbs and descents but basically the road follows the Bow River and railroad line and climbs gradually from Banff at 1,383 meters to Lake Louise at 1,536 meters. The road is narrow, but traffic is both light and usually not in a hurry. A good food stop and hiking area is the Johnston Canyon at 27 km. Most impressive are Castle Mountain with its distinctive horizontal rock layering and, near Lake Louise, the very much more tectonically-disturbed Temple Mountain. The Bow Valley Parkway ends at the road to the Lake Louise Ski Area, Whitehorn Road. Turn left. Lake Louise Village is 1 km downhill and over the bridge across Highway 1.

Sampson Mall in Lake Louise Village has shops and restaurants for almost every need and want. My favorite is Laggan's Mountain Bakery and Deli. A rewarding but tough side trip is the ride up the busy road to Lake Louise Chateau and the lake itself, a 5 km climb of about 200 meters. An obscure gravel bike path also goes there but is somewhat difficult to find, so the choice is between a busy road and a rough path. A third option is to save the Chateau and Lake for the return trip (day 12) and do the busy road as a quick downhill. Another possible side trip is the ride to Moraine Lake in the Valley of the Ten Peaks, about 12 km one way and also uphill.

North of Lake Louise, the route is about 2 km of the busy Trans-Canada Highway and then turns off onto the Icefields Parkway towards Bow Pass and eventually Jasper. Even with the views of the impressive Temple Mountain area behind, the climb is not steep with an elevation gain of only about 290 meters in the 20 km to the Mosquito Creek Hostel.

The hostel has food items for sale or groceries can be carried from Lake Louise.

Day 2 - Mosquito Creek to Beauty Creek - 120 km (Maps 7-11)

This is a relatively long day with two mountain passes. However, the first comes early and is an easy effort. The day starts with the rest of the climb past Crowfoot Glacier and Bow Lake to Bow Pass. This is a gradual elevation gain of 240 meters in 26 km. The first time up here in 1973 surprised us with the sign that we had reached the pass. "Like that's it"? A side trip at the pass is the short but steep road to the Peyto Lake overlook, about 1.5 km to the upper parking lot and well worth the effort. Caution is justified on the return back down.

The road continuing north from Bow Pass starts as a steep downhill, and then the grade eases past Mistaya and Waterfowl Lakes and towering Mount Chephren. It is 25 km to the Saskatchewan River Crossing, which is 620 meters lower in elevation. The Crossing is a tourist center 2 km uphill from the river bridge and a natural place for a break. The Pub restaurant in the hotel behind the souvenir and cafeteria building is recommended. The climbing continues as the route is now approaching notorious Sunwapta Pass. It is easy going along the Saskatchewan River for about 28 km passing the Rampart Creek Hostel and the Weeping Wall series of waterfalls. Then things get interesting.

A steep stretch of about 1 km takes the road up to the Nigel Creek Bridge with a view of the cars and campers straight ahead and high up at the overlook on the side of Parker Ridge. After the bridge, the grade eases on a swing around a broad loop on top of glacial debris from the unseen Saskatchewan Glacier. The road then swings close to Parker Ridge and resumes serious climbing. The overlook is a good place to catch your breath and take pictures of the valley of the Saskatchewan and Nigel River Bridge below. Parker Ridge has a long exposure of curving rock layers called a syncline and shows the dramatic effects of compressive tectonic forces. The parking lot a short way beyond the overlook is a good place to rest and take the short hike to view Panther Falls.

After the overlook, the road curves right back to the northwest and continues the steep climb for about two km. Then it gradually eases in grade as it passes through a high alpine area with patches of snow at road level. The Hilda Creek Hostel is high up near the pass and, three km later, there's the pyramid-like marker that indicates the boundary between Banff and Jasper Parks. The pass elevation sign was a traditional group picture site marking that the major challenge of the trip was met. The sign was missing on the 2001 trip. Sunwapta Pass is 2,035 meters, 644 meters higher than the Saskatchewan River Crossing.

The next milestone is the Columbia Icefield Center, another two km north and surrounded by mountains sporting thick snowcaps and glaciers. Most imposing is the Athabasca Glacier which slopes up the valley to the Columbia Icefield on the horizon. The short ride and hike to the glacier's toe area is worthwhile. Visitors can hike on the tear ice, but caution is justified as it contains crevasses where water can be heard running below. Yearly date markers document the glacier's retreat since its discovery.

The route is down hill from the Icefield all the way to Jasper 105 km distant and 972 meters lower in elevation. But first, there's a small climb to another parking lot and overlook where the road's serpentine descent into the Sunwapta River Valley can be seen to the north. The view back towards the south used to include the tip of the Athabasca Glacier; however, because it is shrinking, it was not visible in 2001. Descending to the Sunwapta Valley requires caution. The road is steep and curvy, and can have gusty winds. One bicycle tour company had a client crash on this downhill while we were there in 1995. Once down to river level, it is easy riding to Beauty Creek Hostel, 19 km from the Icefield Center.

Day 3 - Beauty Creek to Athabasca Falls - 54 km (Maps 11-12)

This is a "rest day" compared to the previous one. Other than a few small bumps, the route continues downhill along the Sunwapta and Athabasca Rivers. The river is on the left and the Endless Chain Mountain on the right en route to the Sunwapta Falls Resort with its restaurant and gift shop at 30 km. This is a good place, and in fact the only place, for a lunch break. Food can be purchased to take to Athabasca Falls Hostel for the evening, but the hostel does have some food items for sale. A 1-km side trip to Sunwapta Falls is worthwhile. From there it's another 26 km to the Athabasca Falls Hostel past imposing Mt. Kerkeslin. After arriving and unloading gear, a good afternoon or evening activity is the walk across the road to Athabasca Falls. There are restrooms there but no other facilities.

Day 4 - Athabasca Falls to Maligne Canyon - 43 km (Maps 13-16)

The route to Maligne Canyon first goes to the town of Jasper, and there are two choices: the main road (Highway 93) and the narrow old road (Highway 93A). The old road is tougher as it first climbs about 100 meters to the Mt. Edith Cavell Road junction and then starts its serious descent to Jasper. It is, of course, less traveled and has another benefit - resident bear or bears usually spotted near the junction. Either way, Jasper is 32 km and a good place to eat, shower, do laundry if needed, shop, and just hang around.

The 11-km or so ride from Jasper to the Maligne Canyon Hostel also has route options but, in any case, finishes with a climb on the Maligne Canyon Road of about 110 meters. The simple route goes north on Jasper's main street, Connaught Drive, to Highway 16 where it continues north 2 km to the bridge across the Athabasca River. After you cross the bridge and bear left, the Hostel is 7 km uphill just past the Maligne River bridge. There is a nice overlook of Jasper on the climb just short of the hostel. There is also a tea house across the road from the hostel as well as the canyon with its interpretative walk.

The other route option from Jasper is a scenic one through the Jasper Park Lodge grounds (Maps 16 and 17). From downtown, Hazel Ave. (also Highway 93A) crosses the railroad tracks, Highway 16, and then goes to Old Fort Road (a left turn). Old Fort Road dead ends shortly after the Athabasca River bridge but bikes can continue.

After circling Lake Beauvert, the route continues north either to the north exit of the Lodge grounds, or via roads and paths east of Lake Edith, to intercept the Maligne Canyon Road.

Day 5 - Hanging around Maligne Canyon, biking and/or hiking (Maps 14-17)

This is a "rest day." There are many options for resting. One is to ride up the Maligne Lake Road to either Medicine Lake (26 km round trip) or to the road's end at the Maligne Lake Center (74 km round trip). This trip is not terribly restful with a total climb of 516 meters. However, it is very scenic at Maligne Lake and around Medicine Lake as well. Other things to do are to ride or hike back into Jasper, take the Jasper Tramway up on Whistler Mountain, explore the Lodge grounds, do the Maligne Canyon hike (if not done the day before), none, some, or all of the above.

Day 6 - Maligne Canyon to Mt. Edith Cavell - 34 km (Maps 13-15)

This seems a short day but can be a full one, especially if the climb to the Whistler Mountain Tram and tram ride are included. In any event, the planning should include food shopping in Jasper and carrying those supplies to Mt. Edith Cavell. The total climb from Jasper is 700 meters, the last 13 km on a switchback and bumpy, although paved, Mt. Edith Cavell road. On July 21, 2001, the hostel manager said the eight of us were this season's second through ninth bikers to visit! The hostel with its high mountain setting is unquestionably worth the effort and has been part of all seven trips I've done there between 1973 and 2001.

The itinerary is to return to Jasper and then depart to the south on Highway 93 retracing the route, in reverse, of two days earlier. At 6 km, take Highway 93A, uphill of course, to the Mt. Edith Cavell Road junction. There begins the switchbacked climb. Look out for the resident bear(s) at the junction.

The mountains up at the hostel press in so closely in air so clear it looks like you could reach out and touch them. The hostel is about 2 km short of the end of the road, where there's an interpretive hike to Cavell Glacier and its lake of icebergs below the towering rock face of Mt. Edith Cavell and Angel Glacier. A teahouse was there at one time but now there's just a parking lot, restrooms, and one incredible view.

Day 7 - Mt. Edith Cavell to Beauty Creek - 88 km (Maps 11-13)

The tour is returning south redoing the roads ridden on the way to Jasper. The views and experiences will be different, however, as will the diversion to Yoho Park in British Columbia. This has been my plan on all my seven trips and no one has ever called it "boring."

This is an easy day overall. The bumpy descent back down the Mt. Edith Cavell road is mostly a test of brakes, and caution is justified. As you continue south on Highway 93A toward its junction of Highway 93 (Icefields Parkway), the view ahead is dominated by Mount Fryatt. When clear, this makes a good photo backdrop with a mild telephoto lens. Moose and elk are often seen on this stretch. Once you are on Highway 93, the gradual ascent begins alongside, first, the Athabasca River, and then, the Sunwapta River. A few short steep climbs help keep the blood warm. First chance for lunch is Sunwapta Falls at 55 km and then it is another 32 km to the Beauty Creek Hostel.

Day 8 - Beauty Creek to Rampart Creek - 56 km (Maps 9-11)

This is a short but challenging day over Sunwapta Pass and, like day 2, one of the best bike rides one can do. It starts with an easy warm up for what's to come. The road grade is so gradually uphill as to be unnoticeable except for the oncoming Sunwapta River meandering over coarse old glacial debris. At about 11 km, the climb gets serious enough for nothing else to be noticed. The Tangle Creek Falls is passed, better appreciated on this ascent than it was as a blur on the downhill run six days earlier. After grinding it out in granny gear through the rock cut, you reach the viewpoint and then the short descent to the Icefields Center and an expensive cafeteria lunch.

The rest of the day is easy, a ride in the park, so to speak. The downhill to the Saskatchewan River is expected to be fast and exciting and is, in part. However, descending bikers rounding the curve at the Saskatchewan Valley overlook are impacted by a sudden brisk headwind off the unseen Saskatchewan Glacier to the west, previously shielded by Parker Ridge. It's still a coast, but much of the speed is lost. The descent after the Nigel Creek bridge is better but can be scary if traffic is heavy. This is the only part of the Icefields Parkway that does not have a full-width shoulder. Past the Weeping Wall, the riding is easy except for one small climb approaching Rampart Creek.

Dinner can be a problem at Rampart Creek unless the hostel now stocks food. Ask about this when making reservations. Other options are to send the strongest riders on a shopping trip to the Crossing, about 22 km round trip, or carry food from the Columbia Icefield Center.

Day 9 - Rampart Creek to Mosquito Creek - 62 km (Maps 7-9)

This day could be combined with the previous one, as we did for our 2001 tour. It makes a challenging 122 km with two hard passes, but it's not unmanageable for well-prepared bikers. It simplifies the problem of obtaining food.

As with the previous two days, this one gives riders an easy warmup. The Crossing at 11 km is the only place for lunch. From there, the climbing starts towards Bow Pass 25 km away and 620 m higher in elevation. This climb is not as trivial as was the one over Bow Pass from the south. It warrants some kind of energy snack for the approach or at least a celebration at the top. Once you are over the pass on the south side, the views of Bow Peak, Crowfoot Glacier and later Bow Lake make spectacular backdrops for photos of bike tourists on the road. It's then an easy 26 km downhill to the Mosquito Creek Hostel. The hostel has food for sale, or a shopping run could be made to Lake Louise (40 km round trip).

Day 10 - Mosquito Creek to Whiskey Jack - 66k (Maps 6-7)

This day is another spectacular mountain experience which includes Kicking Horse Pass at the Continental Divide between Alberta and British Columbia. The start is a steady downhill for 17 km to the termination of Icefields Parkway at Highway 1 (just north of Lake Louise Village). Turning right (west) onto Highway 1 takes the rather trivial climb to the Divide which is only about a 110-meter ascent in 6 km. The road follows and crisscrosses the railroad, Canada's first to the west coast. West Louise Lodge and restaurant are 5 km west of, but still high up on, the pass. It is the only place, and fortunately a good place, for a lunch stop.

From there, the road begins down, passes the railroad's spiral tunnel overlook, and drops 400 meters to the turnoff for the Yoho Valley. The concern here is food for the overnight or two expected at the

Whiskey Jack Hostel in Yoho Park. The town of Field is 3 km west of the turnoff (out of the way) and has a small although decent store and cafe. There is no noticeable climbing on this detour to Field as the valley of the Kicking Horse River is essentially flat there. The other option is the smaller store at the Cathedral Mountain Chalets on the way up the Yoho Valley Road. It is not unusual to find someone going up to Takakkaw Falls who will take the food up for the group and drop it off at the hostel.

The 13-km, 250-meter climb to the hostel has some tough stretches. A set of sharp switchbacks requires tour buses to do one part in reverse gear. The last climb right before the hostel brings the biker to the awesome sight of, first Takakkaw Falls and, then, the valley of the Yoho Glacier. A similar but closer view is also available from the hostel porch. As a significant and warm realization, the hostel also has hot showers and flush toilets.

Day 11 - Hanging around Whiskey Jack, hiking for sure

The narrow Yoho valley was down-cut by a glacier and is lined by hanging valleys and waterfalls. Hiking is the best activity there as biking options are limited to riding back down the Yoho Valley. An easy hike is up the Yoho Valley. However, a spectacular hike is the Iceline Trail, which ascends a series of switchbacks just behind the hostel. This trail approaches the Emerald Glacier on the Presidential Range and has views across the valley to the Daly Glacier, down on Takakkaw Falls, and towards the valley's south end with Wapta and Cathedral Mountains and the Trans-Canada Highway climbing towards the Divide. The return via Laughing Falls and the valley trail is a total hike of 17 km. The return via the Whaleback and Twin Falls adds about 7 km more and going up the Little Yoho about 4 more. The Iceline Trail hike is rated among the best in the world.

Day 12 - Whiskey Jack to Castle Mountain - 62 km (Maps 5-6)

The day starts downhill back down the Yoho Valley and includes the set of sharp switchbacks. Use caution. After you exit the Yoho Valley, there then is the climb on Highway 1 back up to Kicking Horse Pass. Although not trivial at 400 meters, it seems to always be accompanied by tailwinds (from the west) and is not as steep as, for example, Sunwapta or the north side of Bow Pass. This day's ride provides the best opportunity to visit Lake Louise (Lake and Chateau). Two km after Wapta Lake and the West Louise Lodge is the turnoff (right) to Lake O'Hara. This is also the turnoff for the old highway (1A) which, by 2001, was closed to cars and designated as a bikepath. It passes the Continental Divide at a spot which shows the division of the waters and continues on to join the road to Lake Louise just 1 km below the Chateau and Lake. Turn right and bike uphill. After that visit, group photo and whatever, it is an exciting 195-meter descent to Lake Louise Village.

The rest of the ride to Castle Mountain involves taking the village road towards and over Highway 1, continuing uphill 1 km on Whitehorn Road (route to Lake Louise Ski Area), and turning right onto the Bow Valley Parkway (Highway 1A). It's all downhill from there.

Groceries are available across the road from the hostel at Castle Mountain Village and meals are available at Johnston Canyon Resort about 6 km south on 1A.

Day 13 - Castle Mountain to Banff - 33 km (Map 4)

The route continues down the Bow Valley Parkway past Johnston Canyon and to the Junction with Highway 1. Since this is a short day, there is opportunity to do touristy things that may have been missed earlier such as the Johnston Canyon hike and the various options in and around Banff. It could also be a chance to get a start on heading home. After nearly two weeks in the mountains, bustling Banff may seem inharmonious. Welcome back to civilization.

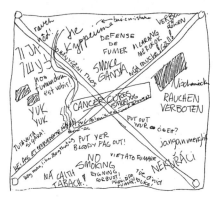

No SMOKING sign, Whiskey Jack.

TOP
Jon Grinols on Bow Valley Parkway in 1973.
BOTTOM
1973 Minnesota AYH group, sans Charley, at the
Athabasca Falls Hostel. L to R: Roy, Bette, Jacque, Vic, Laurie, Dee,
Frank, Bob, Jon, and the author

Charley Field, Jacque Lindskoog, and Jon Grinols in 1973,
At the Saskatchewan River Crossing.

TOP
1975 Minnesota AYH group at the Athabasca Falls Hostel. L to R:
Sylvia, the author, hostel manager (with two children), Dave
Kvistberg, Laurie, Jacque, Wayne and Jerry.
BOTTOM
Columbia Icefield Chalet in 1975.

Wayne Lindskoog admiring mother bear with two cubs,
somewhere along the Icefields Parkway, 1975.

TOP
Most of 1982 group at the Hector Lake overlook,
Icefields Parkway. L to R: Marilyn and Jon Grinols, Lisa, Sylvia, Sara
and Doug Laird and Joann and Fred Armbruster.
BOTTOM
Daniel Siskind, age 11, and goats on Sunwapta Pass, 1982.

Lisa, age 14, Sylvia, and Daniel, age 11, departing the
Lake Louise area on the Icefields Parkway, 1982.

ABOVE
Dana Siskind and a Whisky
Jack (Canadian Gray Jay)
at the Peyto Lake overlook
on Bow Pass, in 1986.
Note: Parks Canada
discourages the
feeding of wildlife.
Dana is trying to explain
this to bird.

LEFT
Theresa Scanlan and mom,
Dana Siskind, on the
Johnston Canyon hike, 1986.

Dana and Theresa on the Sunwapta Pass climb, Banff Park side, 198
Nigel Creek bridge is visible below.

TOP
Banff townsite from Sulphur Mountain.
BOTTOM
Elizabeth, age 11, leading Marcy, Dana, and Gary in 1991.

TOP
Tandem team, Ruth and John Long in 1991.
BOTTOM
Dana and Elizabeth in 1991.

TOP
Most of 1991 group at Sunwapta Pass elevation sign.
BOTTOM
Dana and Elizabeth admiring Rocky Mountain sheep, 1991.

TOP
Tony and Jodi at Saskatchewan River, 1991.
BOTTOM
Mount Edith Cavell visible beyond Jasper Park Lodge gate.

Switchbacks on Yoho Valley road, 1991.

TOP
Marcy, Dana, Pat, Elizabeth, and Gary saying their goodbys to
Mosquito Creek Hostel Manager, Tony Chatham, 1995.
BOTTOM
Sauna at Mosquito Creek Hostel, 1995.

TOP
Hiking the cliffs above the Rampart Creek Hostel, 1995.
BOTTOM
Hikers on the Athabasca Glacier near the Icefield Center, 1995.

Boundary marker between Banff and Jasper National Parks, and
Patrick, 1995.

ABOVE
Elizabeth and Dana
approaching Bow Pass
from the north, 1995.
LEFT
Leaving Sunwapta Falls
rest stop, heading south,
1995.

ABOVE
Catching up to Japanese
biker and soon-to-be
dinner guest, 1995.

LEFT
Cute but not feedable.

TOP
Marcy hiking high above the Yoho Valley and Takakkaw Falls,1995.
BOTTOM
The Iceline Trail on the Vice President Range, Yoho Park, 1995.

1995 tour ready to depart from Whiskey Jack Hostel in Yoho Park. Up the steps: Gary, Elizabeth (15 years), Patrick, the author, Marcy, Olga (the hostel manager), and Dana.

TOP
North Star Ski Touring Club trip, sans Eva, in front of
Banff International Hostel, 2001. L to R: Marv, Kitty, Melissa, Ed,
Jim, Scott, Tom, and the author.
BOTTOM
Four of the guys on Highway 93A near Athabasca Falls, 2001.

ABOVE
Jim Nelson
approaching
Athabasca Glacier and
Icefield Center, 2001.

LEFT
Tom, Scott, Author, and
Jim in Kananaskis
Country en route to
Banff, 2001.

ABOVE
Jim near Bow Pass on
Icefields Parkway,
2001.

LEFT
Author facing
Sunwapta Pass from
near Beauty Creek,
Jasper Park, 2001.

TOP
Six of the nine 2001 tour bikers at Lake Louise, Eva, Kitty, Marv, Jim, Tom, and the author
BOTTOM
The same six getting ready to depart Whiskey Jack Hostel and Manager Olga in Yoho National Park, 2001.

Chapter 7

Seven Stories of Bicycling the Canadian Rockies

1973 - FINALLY, TRAVELING WITH CHARLEY

"Who are those guys"? His reply was, "Haven't you heard, they are the Minnesota Ironmen" and then he saw me and "here's one of them now." I was too surprised at this Lone Ranger imitation (Who was that masked man?) to respond, much less deny anything. Our group of 11 riders in patriotic, for Canada, red and white Lambertini jerseys had come down from the Mt. Edith Cavell Hostel and were passing the Athabasca Falls Hostel enroute to distant Rampart Creek. I stopped in to see if I had left a pair of shorts there from four days previous, and there was a group still milling about prior to starting their day (the 43rd Street Y of NYC, I think). At the hostel was someone we had met the week before and had obviously impressed. The "Ironmen" comment surprised me though. It must have come from the embroidered patches on some of our handlebar bags from the annual Minnesota Ironman century ride. I never heard us say we were "ironmen," but it would have been hard to deny we made no secret of our long daily miles and traveling without sleeping bags.

I was leading a Minnesota Council American Youth Hostel (AYH) trip through the most dramatic and beautiful scenery in North America, the Canadian Rocky Mountain National Parks of Banff, Jasper, and Yoho. For all of us, me included, it was our first time there. Some car tourists had told us how sorry they felt for us, seeing us biking up steep Sunwapta Pass. The reality was that we were loving it. We couldn't imagine experiencing these mountains any better way than from our bikes. Bike nuts on tour. Riding mountains can be wearing but can also bring on the highest of highs for it's where the scenery and the the endorphins meet. This seems especially so in these beautiful but eminently bikeable Canadian Rockies National Parks in Alberta and British Columbia. Biking and hiking these parks are so exciting and rewarding that I have been back to them six more times at about five-year intervals between 1973 and 2001 and will surely return again.

I had biked in the mountains before Banff and had considered them "real enough" at the time. First time was as a teenaged biker on a 1961 Cycling Enthusiast of Philadelphia Club trip to the Poconos in Pennsylvania. Following that were the Appalachian mountains of North Jersey from 1962 to 1965, and later one tough ride on Virginia's Skyline Drive with Washington, D.C. Cycling friend Bill Vetter in 1967.

The Penn State campus in State College, PA provided a serious escalation in mountain bicycling. These were longer and higher climbs on regular bike club and solo rides my 5-1/2 years there between 1964 and 1970. Penn State University's main campus is in the valley and ridge province of the Appalachian Mountains, including the Nittany Valley where prowls the famous Penn State Nittany lion. The less challenging rides stay the valleys or cross through the ancient uplifted ridges through old river gaps. Such were the rides to Milheim, Penn's Cave, Centennial, and Tyrone. Tougher rides required at least one crossing from one valley to another with a one- to two-mile muscle burning climbs at grades of about 10 percent. These were rides to Altoona, Tylerville, Huntington, up and over Bald Eagle Mountain and onto the Allegheny Plateau including Snow Shoe, Black Moshannon, Romona, and Clearfield. In my exuberant youth and love of my brand new Schwinn Paramount track bike (crazy idiot is more like it), I did many of these on a fixed gear powering up in either a 70-inch gear (50-20) and trying not to get spun out on the descents. I can still remember the climbs, but will *never* forget those descents. Later, I bought two old road bikes from Philadelphia friend Fred Breida and took this terrain a little more sensibly.

But even with five years in the Appalachians, I think of the Canadian Rockies as my first real mountains, specifically, the four National Parks that Canada has created to protect them: Banff, Jasper, Yoho and Kootenay. I had lots of concerns on my first trip there, leading a Minnesota AYH group. I wasn't sure how we prairie riders would handle these "real" mountains and apprehensive of the weather we'd encounter. Aside from a two-person, one week, somewhat-of-a-fiasco Philadelphia to Washington, D.C. tour about 10 years earlier, it was my first experience as a tour leader and only my third time on any kind of bike tour. I planned all the details and how they would be carried out. We were all well prepared. Even more so, although with little rationale, I felt responsible for everyone having good time. On a tour, the leader does what he can hoping everyone realizes that some factors are not predictable or controllable. In theory, everyone buys into the trip realizing that.

George Colerich of the Minnesota AYH had shown me a National Geographic article about Banff Park in the Canadian Rockies, suggesting I lead a Minnesota Council AYH trip there in 1973. George had been leading regular Minnesota Council trips to Europe. One photo in particular sold me: an aerial view of the Banff town site from Sulphur mountain showing rugged peaks rising dramatically around the compact town. I started researching hostel locations, terrain, food sources, and a potential itinerary for a two -week trip that would include Banff, Jasper, and Yoho Parks. We were to drive out in Bob Remington's van, pulling a trailer of bikes. The regional Youth Hostel office in Calgary, 80 miles east of the Banff town site, provided a place to park our van and trailer. Our group, averaging 31 years in age, was very strong, with most having done the Minnesota AYH Paul Bunyan double-century ride the week before. Long mileages were scheduled and reservations made for the overnights, all of which would be in hostels except for the drive out and back, two days each way.

We had two incredible weeks of "wow, look at that", thinking this must be the most scenic ride in North America. Every view had rocky , snowy peaks, forested slopes, and mountain lakes or rivers. The mountains rose suddenly from the valleys with no gradual foothills. Even though most topped out at a relatively low 10,000-ft (3,000 meters), they looked rugged and dramatic. We took the old highway from Banff to the Lake Louise area, Bow Valley Parkway aka Highway 1A, and then the Icefields Parkway to Jasper. There are high mountains on both sides as the road climbs over easy Bow Pass and then along lakes and rivers to much more challenging and dramatic Sunwapta Pass. Hanging glaciers are all along the western side range, and the Columbia Icefield is awesome. From there it is 60 miles and 3,000 feet of downhill to the Jasper town site. Our Lambertini trip jerseys were Canadian colors - white stripes on a field of red - and looked glorious under the bright sun and clear blue skies.

This, our first Canadian Rockies trip had 11 riders: Bob Remington, Frank Braun (an experienced AYH tripper), John Grinols, Vic Grevious, Roy Martin, Jacque Lindskoog (later to be our famous

American Birkenbeiner skier, Hawaii Ironman finisher, and Odyssey 2000 rider), Dee Boeck, Laurie Affield, Bette Nelson, and Charley Field. We all went out in the van except Charley, who flew out. He had his bike with him, luckily. I had screwed up the rendezvous, and Charley ended up chasing after us through the parks for five days. The first day we rode to Spray River Hostel, three miles past the Banff town site (88 miles), and just upstream from the huge Banff Springs Hotel. The next day it was past Lake Louise and over easy Bow Pass to Rampart Creek Hostel for a century day. In doing this, we bypassed three hostels as being just not far enough. Skipping hostels would be typical of this trip as some were as close as 20 miles apart. We knew right away we were in for an incredible experience even if some things weren't perfect. We wondered where Charley was, how we were going to stay warm enough without sleeping bags, and how to handle the grief Bob was giving hostel managers about the hostels not being clean enough. It was hard to keep from laughing when genuine anger is combined with the words "dust bunnies." Although Bob was right that the hostels could have been cleaner, complaining about it was not really constructive. The idea of giving guests clean - up chores did not seem to work in a situation where both hosts and guests were transients.

In talking with other hostel stayers, we downplayed our long days and lack of sleeping bags as we were "tough Minnesotans". We rode inhuman miles (e.g., skipping hostels) over mountains, we slept in the cold, and we used spokes for toothpicks, etc. We didn't realize we were creating a legend ("Who are those guys?"). Charley later told us he was hearing stories about us at every hostel as he pursued us up the Icefields Parkway. We saw everything there was to see in the Jasper area, staying at the Athabasca Falls, Maligne Canyon, and Mt. Edith Cavell hostels. Charley caught up with us at Mt. Edith Cavell making the group whole. We swapped a lot of stories with Charley. The big difference was he knew we were ahead, but his appearance at Mt. Edith Cavell was a surprise to us, a happy one. I felt many emotions: relieved, stupid, and guilty. He was very gracious in not giving me the chewing out I deserved.

One trip story was about the peanut butter sandwich. We had been eating our absolute fills at every meal, all of us being ravenous with the exercise and mountain air. We left Rampart Creek for the easy 12-mile warm-up before the steep climb up Sunwapta Pass with our as-usual full "tanks." Nobody wanted the odd left over sandwich, so Jacque took it along. Part way up Sunwapta, she pulled out the sandwich and there was almost a fight for it. It was amazing how so much hunger could develop in so short a time.

These parks are still wilderness despite the heavy tourism. There are signs warning of bear encounters, stating that you should "stay in your vehicle." That would be a cool trick for bicyclists. We saw a mother black bear with a cub at the Mt. Edith Cavell road junction. They crossed the road in front of us. We again saw this pair as we turned the second switchback on the climb, this time below us. The cub scrambled up a tree while mother watched us. We would see bears at or near this junction on most of our trips. We also saw moose, and I recall watching Bob Remington chase one enormous male into the woods in an attempt to get a good picture. I wondered if this was wise, but by that time I was afraid to advise Bob on anything. Near Whiskey Jack Hostel in Yoho we saw another moose calmly munching the grass just off the road. Jacque said, "Let's get closer." When the moose eyed us from about 10 feet away I said, "Lets not." We were later told he's the "resident moose" of the area. There are elk everywhere in both Banff and Jasper towns, sometimes eating grass on residential lawns and golf courses. Sheep and goats also grazed along the roadway.

Banff and Jasper are in Alberta on the eastern side of the Continental Divide while Yoho Park is is an easy ride over the divide to British Columbia. I had deliberately saved the side trip to Yoho for the return south, wanting to keep the return to Banff and the trip's end from being an anticlimax. To get to Yoho, we climbed Kicking Horse Pass with its dramatic dual spiral railroad tunnels, and on the return two days later we took the old road, Highway 1A, and visited Lake Louise with it's big Chateau. The road up the dramatically narrow Yoho valley was steep, with a tight pair of unpaved switch backs where the relatively few tourist buses had to climb the middle stretch in reverse. We scheduled a day off in Yoho Park for hiking, as we had at lofty Mt. Edith Cavell. Most of us walked the 15-mile valley trail round trip to the teahouse, while some made it there via the more exciting Whaleback or Highline routes, which overlook the glacial valley. Just sitting on the porch at Yoho's Whiskey Jack Hostel in Yoho was a treat. We had the nearby thundering 1,000-ft Takakkaw Falls and the Yoho Glacier at the end of the valley.

Busy and bustling Banff town seemed unsettling and less appealing than the first time through, after 10 days in the beautiful mountain wilderness. At least our scattered around bike group could easily be spotted in their red and white biking jerseys. Costs were low for this trip. We did group cooking plus two celebration restaurant dinners. Twelve days of hostel overnights and meals cost only $75 despite the high food costs in the parks. Those riding the van from Minneapolis to Calgary and back contributed an additional $30 for those expenses.

Without intending to, we got back to Calgary one day early. Our last "official" overnight was at Ribbon Creek Hostel up the Kananaskis Highway between Banff and Calgary. It was a 28 -mile round trip off the Trans-Canada Highway but the road surface was large loose rocks. The group consensus was to skip this hostel even though it meant foregoing 11 prepaid reservations. We continued straight into Calgary and chalked up another long day at 101 miles. At the end-of-trip steak-house celebration dinner, Vic, our only underage at 17, sat at one end of the table and acted as one of the wine approvers. After watching Charley's performance, Vic did it perfectly as the rest of us all smiled.

This trip was close to perfect. Our few errors were not bringing sleeping bags, (except for Roy who was biking all the way back to the Twin Cities), and possibly having some too-long days. My own additional error was not remembering accurately where we were suppose to meet Charley. Starting our mountain experiences in Banff, rather in Jasper, allowed us to warm up on easy Bow Pass ("You mean that's it"?) rather than having to do tougher Sunwapta first. Banff is also at a higher elevation than Jasper, giving us an easier first week. On later trips, the option of starting in Jasper had some travel advantages, but would still have a rougher trip warmup. The highest elevation we reached was 6,700 feet (2,100 meters) so we weren't faced with altitude sickness or any noticeable acclimation problems. The hostels were quaint and friendly places to meet other travelers, although not as clean as we were used to (dust bunnies), nor did they all have sufficient blankets as we had expected. We were always able to find food for cooking even if it meant carrying it a ways on our bikes, buying "ingredients" from restaurants and planning the meals while in the process of shopping. "Okay, what do they have and what are our options?" For the lack of sleeping bags, we piled all our clothes on us. It all worked out. It usually does.

1975 - TOURING COUPLES

We knew an encore to the Canadian Rockies was inevitable, but wife Sylvia and I used our summer of 1974 for a six week tour of Europe. The Minnesota AYH Council did run a trip that year, which included Burt Swan, John Roberts, and Bill Hamilink. The next year, 1975, looked feasible for a return trip for most of the 1973 group, plus sharing it with spouses. Besides Sylvia and me, Jacque Lindskoog brought husband Wayne, Laurie Afield brought fiancé Jerry Hoffman, and the group was rounded out by an old friend and regular Twin Cities area biker Dave Kvistberg, seven of us in all. Charley Field had wanted to go but was sidelined by a medical problem. Dave Kvistberg had also just recovered from being sick and was a little concerned about his fitness for touring. The Minnesota AYH actually ran three Canadian Rockies trips in 1975. One was led by Frank Braun and we met up with them at the foot of the climb to Mt. Edith Cavell. A third trip in August included Mike Ruedy and Burt Swan.

Our trip formula was similar to that of 1973, but this time we started and ended the tour in Banff instead of Calgary. Knocking off this 170 miles allowed us to eliminate the century days and add a few hostels. Jacque, Wayne, and Dave Kvistberg took the VIA Rail's *Canadian,* from Winnipeg directly to the Banff train station. Laurie and Jerry needed inexpensive transportation so they went out with Sylvia and me in our car. We parked in Canmore and biked the short distance into the park and to the Spray River Hostel near Banff. Unfortunately, there is no longer regular train service directly to Banff. The cross-Canada trains now go farther north through Edmonton and Jasper.

Our first day's ride to Lake Louise was less than 40 miles. Some of us added to it by doing the side trip to Moraine Lake and the Valley of the Ten Peaks. Early the next day, Kvistberg broke a pedal between Lake Louise and Bow Pass. He had to return to Banff for a replacement while the rest of us went on. For part of this, luckily, he was able to hop a bus. We waited and worried about him at Rampart Creek while climbing around on the cliffs behind the hostel. Fortunately, it stays light until nearly midnight at that latitude in early July, for he arrived at 10 p.m., pretty exhausted.

We enjoyed the trappings of civilization in Jasper town: sitting in the park, people watching, hot showers (finally) and laundry at the public laundromat, and of course, shopping for food and souvenirs. This trip had lots of rain and at other times lots of heat, up to 97 degrees. One time, Sylvia, Dave, and I took shelter from a rain shower not realizing that we were only a couple of hundred feet from the Athabasca Falls Hostel. Later, we got quite soaked en route to Rampart Creek on the southbound return and then watched the NYC group arrive, also soaked. While trying to dry out all our stuff and having dinner in the kitchen/common cabin, we heard the hostel manager yell out from her cabin's little porch "*Close your door*"! A bear was prowling around the hostel buildings. Not able to get to our food, he crossed the road to the campground and fed himself there. As on all the trips to these parks, we saw bears, elk, sheep, goats, and sometimes moose, porcupines, bear cubs, and cats.

I was able to hike the Highline (now "Iceline") trail in Yoho Park with most of the group, unlike in 1973, when I had to return early for cooking duty. This hike was spectacular, with a series of switchbacks behind the hostel taking us well above Takakkaw Falls and Daly Glacier which feeds the falls. We hiked in the rock breakdown just below the glacier on the Vice President Range to the river above Twin Falls near the teahouse. The man-made bridge there was missing so we crossed on the snow bridge. Later, we met a ranger who asked how we got there and chewed us out because a collapse of the snow could have had serious, maybe even fatal, consequences. In retrospect, crossing this way without a rope for safety was not smart but the snow seemed firm and even had some pretty big rocks imbedded in it.

Although still a great trip, I had some frustration with the interpersonal aspects. The coupling up created little "cliques," and we didn't gel together as well as in 1973. It also wasn't a new place as it had been two years earlier. The weather was worse and the parks seemed more crowded. Dave Kvistberg wasn't his usual strong self and I was sorry Charley Field couldn't make it. We sat next to the river at the Beauty Creek Hostel and shared a bottle of wine called Lonesome Charley. In an unlikely coincidence, the bottle's label had a bike on it. I guess mostly, I missed the bright sun and blue skies of the previous trip.

1982 - KIDS CAN DO THIS

In a Banff town restaurant the night before the 1982 trip start: Doug said, "I think I'll have another glass of milk as I don't know if we'll eat well the next two weeks." It wasn't to be a problem. We found advance planning to be useless, but we always found enough of what passed for food and nobody went hungry. It was seven years later, July 1982, and we were back for Canadian Rockies, Edition III. This and later Canadian Rockies bike trips were on a family plan; distances suitable for well prepared kids of 11 years and older. We had 10 riders altogether, my wife Sylvia, daughter Lisa (just turned 14), and son Daniel (11), friends Doug and Sara Laird and Doug's son Doug Jr. (16), Fred and JoAnn Armbruster, and Morgan Nicole. Also joining us for most of our overnights were Jon and Marylin Grinols, on their two-year honeymoon tandem circuit of the USA.

Lisa and Daniel were experienced bikers from trips to Wisconsin's Sparta-Elroy Trail and Minnesota's Heartland Trail, and the previous year's RAGBRAI. They had trained by biking about 1,000 miles in the three months before this trip. That distance was a requirement I put on them, with the constant reminder that they would have to face and conquer the notorious Sunwapta Pass. We and the Lairds were able to take the train this time. At the Banff train station, we met up with the Armbrusters who drove and the Grinols rode in on their tandem.

I was hugely impressed with the kids, our two and Doug Jr., who every day hauled their own coal. They managed the mountain passes and distances with no complaints (well, few complaints; well, they're not complaining about it anymore) and gave me great photo opportunities. Sylvia's Phil Wood bottom bracket loosened on the Sunwapta climb, but we were able to cajole some Locktight from John Grinols. We had a lot of stomach problems among the group and started pre washing dishes and pots in the hostels. On this trip we explored the Jasper Park Lodge and golf course area as the nicest, although not shortest, way from Jasper town site to the Maligne Canyon Hostel.

Neither of my kids biked the climb to the Mt. Edith Cavell Hostel. It was Lisa's day to be sick and Daniel had a sore knee. We got a lift in a car for Lisa, and Daniel went with the Grinols for two days as they declined to take the 450-pound gross weight tandem up the long and switchbacked climb. We all regrouped at the Icefield Chalet two days later. The Hilda Creek Hostel high up and just south of Sunwapta Pass was a bit crowded. They were down to one bunkhouse, the other apparently having been burnt down by visiting British soldiers. I hope the Canadian Youth Hostel Association got reimbursed for that.

Our stay at Whiskey Jack Hostel was not as much fun as in previous years. We were very crowded because another group had delayed their leaving. Worse, it rained all day and we were mostly just lying around, finally getting in a short hike to Laughing Falls late in the day. We didn't laugh much that day. There was snow on the ground the next day when we said goodbye to the Manager, Olga Forbes, and left Whiskey Jack for Kicking Horse Pass and the snowless eastern side of the Continental Divide. The group had broken up in Yoho; John and Marilyn heading west toward Golden, Fred to Banff to pick up the car so JoAnn wouldn't have to strain her acting-up back, and Morgan solo to Banff to get away from the rest of us. We luxuriated at the Banff hot springs before catching the train for Winnipeg and then the drive home.

The Teahouse at Twin Falls.

1986 - EAT AT TONY'S

"Nikon, very good camera." Another Japanese tourist overheard this and chimed in, "Canon, very good camera". At that, Theresa quietly moved away to let them argue it out. We had been hand feeding the Canadian Jays (aka Whiskey Jacks) at the Peyto Lake overlook thrilling bus loads of Japanese and ensuring that we would make many photo appearances in living rooms throughout Japan. One of them noticed Theresa's new Nikon.

It was my fourth Canadian Rockies tour, and it was very different. There were just three of us: me, my new wife Dana of two weeks, and Dana's older daughter Theresa, who just finished high school. For awhile, it looked like others might go, son Daniel and his friend Nick and Theresa's friend Amer. Somehow, it didn't work out for them so the trip only had the three of us. The formula was the same as the trip four years earlier: drive to Winnipeg, train out to Banff, cycle Banff to Jasper, and cycle the return with the usual side trip to Yoho.

As on all previous trips, we stayed at the Spray River Hostel just outside of Banff with the advertisement on the chimney, "Eat at Tony's." Tony Chatham, the Hostel manager, told us that he occasionally has invitational multi course dinners for all interested hostelers who participate in both the preparation and consumption of this multinational event. Unfortunately, it wasn't this day. Tony was running this hostel on our previous visit in 1982 and we would again meet up with him in 1991 and 1995, but not at this hostel.

Banff's Spray River Hostel was to be replaced by a "fancy" one in town. A shame, as the rustic hostels produced a far more homecoming feeling than these new hotel-like dorms. (In 1991, I biked to the site of the Spray River Hostel and found an empty space where it had been. Sad memories. But, there are other opinions on this fancy Banff "International" hostel and the similar new fancy one at Lake Louise town. They are popular and financially successful even if not adhering to the ideal and intent of international hosteling. Once again, my opinions are in the minority, pretty common with Minnesotans.

It was a strange trip, with Dana and me practically on our honeymoon. Theresa was quiet and missing the company of anyone close to her age. She also had trouble on the climbs and was wiped out after each day's ride. The stuff hit the fan in Jasper after four days of riding. Theresa wanted to go home: "Too much riding and too hilly". Her preparation for this trip wasn't much more than a few laps of three-mile circumference Lake Calhoun in Minneapolis. She considered my admonitions to train seriously about as much as most teenagers listen to their bioparents much less future stepparents. Laceless loose shoes and cruising in too-high gears didn't help either. We looked into the means and costs of getting her from Jasper to Minneapolis. In an uncharacteristically tough stance, Dana said Theresa had to finish the trip even if it meant she'd hitchhike from hostel to hostel.

The three easy days in the Jasper area provided Theresa some recovery. She also bought a sketch pad so she could exercise her art interests during rest breaks and also justify having more of them. This was not a sunny blue sky trip, and we had a little rain most days and about 50 miles of road construction. Nevertheless, the return trip down the Icefield Parkway and to Yoho Park went better. Theresa got noticeably stronger as she pedaled and sketched her way through the mountains and valleys.

While at the Whiskey Jack Hostel, Olga told us she had Tony on the radio. He knew we were due at his place in Banff the next day, had one of his "Eat at Tony's" dinners planned, and wanted to know if we were interested. We said "yes" with no hesitation and, the next evening, that was one of the trip highlights. We had lasagna dinner at Tony's Spray River Hostel with 16 new friends. We followed this up with an easy day of riding around Banff town, taking in the hot baths, and riding the lift up Sulfur Mountain. On Sulfur Mountain, the goats attacked us for our lunches. By Yoho I was sure Theresa was glad she hadn't quit, but stubborn teenager, she never admitted it.

The Chimney at Tony's Place.

1991 - WHAT TOUR DID YOU SAY YOU WERE ON?

Tour number 5 continued the tradition of creating new legends. The following, involving two of them, was written for the Loype, the North Star Ski Touring Club (NSSTC) newsletter, about this trip:

"Marcy"? "Gary, what are you doing here"? The "here" in this case was a sauna at an obscure Canadian Youth Hostel in the mountain wilderness of Banff Park, some 1,300 miles from the North Star State (Minnesota). And the "what" is Gary's decision to do the two-week bike tour after all. Gary and Marcy were two of five North Star members (and 9 persons overall) on a "*Dave's Holiday*" tour of the Canadian Rockies. The "what tour..." question in the title was asked by a Yuppie Bicycle Tour rider describing which of the alternative side trip adventures around Jasper he should considering doing. *Dave's* had done them all.

This trip, run as a NSSTC event, included Dana, Dana's youngest daughter Elizabeth (age 11), Marcy Otypka, and, joining us later, Gary Follett. We also had two Minnesota tandem teams: John and Ruth Long (who had just moved to St. Louis, Missouri) and Tony and Jodi Krulc from Virginia, Minnesota. The itinerary had all the usual elements: three parks, two directions, lots of climbs, especially lots of waterfalls (John said too many). Sometimes even the experienced adult riders were tired, especially on the long climb up Sunwapta Pass from the Athabasca River flats and into a stiff head wind. But, how could they complain when a skinny 11-year old girl was along pedaling her own bike with all her stuff and with a smile yet? A two month 1,100-mile training program worked for Elizabeth who sometimes couldn't resist asking if her older sister Theresa had to walk up this or that hill (on the previous tour in 1986). Words for a complaining young motorcycle passenger met at a scenic overlook just prior to the steep part of the Sunwapta Pass, "You don't know what tired is".

The Gary and Marcy on-again, off-again experience caused us much mirth and also some problems too, but, not nearly as many as Gary had. Gary had been included in my trip planning and advanced hostel reservations. When they fought and Gary decided he couldn't do this tour with Marcy, I tried to talk him into not quitting. His decision to drop out also left Marcy with a dilemma about how to get to Banff. Dana, Elizabeth, and I were doing our usual four-day Winnipeg Folk

Music Festival and then driving out from there. The others were not leaving from Minneapolis and couldn't help. The solution was that Marcy went with us to the festival and then on the two-day drive out to Banff. By the time we did all that and our first days ride to the Corral Creek Hostel, we had been away from Minneapolis for six busy days and Marcy's thoughts were likely far from Gary.

Gary, apparently, could think about nothing else and decided he just had to find us and Marcy. But first, he had to find out where we would be because he had tossed away his copy of our trip itinerary. Getting that from our neighbors, he bought an airline ticket, flew to Calgary, rented a car, and sped to Corral Creek and to that sauna door. I had gone to bed and missed the questions and answers, including John's when he slid over to Dana and asked "What's going on"? I also remember being asked. "Guess who's here." When I awoke the next day, I asked whose arm was hanging down from the bunk overhead. Elizabeth said "Gary" and I replied "no" as I couldn't imagine it. Gary wasn't exactly on my mind either and this was too improbable.

Improbable yes, impossible no. It was Gary. His next steps were to get the rental car back to Calgary, rent a bike, buy some panniers and clothes, and catch up with us. We had to move on because of our reservations. He did all he needed the next day including biking 90 miles from Banff to catch us at the Saskatchewan River Crossing. For the car, he trusted a hitchhiker to return it to the Calgary airport. The rental bike was from a Banff bike shop. When Gary returned it and commented it was hard to ride 500 miles without toe clips, the guy asked, "Where have you had been with it"? and was surprised when Gary said something like "Much of Alberta and some of British Columbia." Most rentals are for rides around town, not in two Provinces. I spent the rest of the trip explaining to hostel managers that we had had a cancellation but the cancellation was now canceled. Some had gotten the word and some hadn't but somehow, we all got accommodated. I was a little put out but far more amused at these Gary-caused happenstances.

"You better hug mom, she's been crying" were Elizabeth's words at the Columbia Icefield Chalet after a challenging ride of 73 miles against the wind and up Sunwapta Pass. First, we had descended the bumpy switchback road from Mt. Edith Cavell that morning and then

70

started the long climb from Athabasca Falls to the roof of the Parks, the Columbia Icefield. The headwinds and continual climbing were slowing us, especially Elizabeth, who was, as usual, twiddling along easily and conserving her energy. As the afternoon got late, I suggested that the faster riders go on ahead and we would regroup at the dinner destination, the Icefield Chalet. Dana, Elizabeth, and I stopped briefly at the Beauty Creek Hostel, considering options like stopping for the day there or catching one of the Brewster buses. I had heard that buses will take bicyclists and recalled Dave Kvistberg's experience 16 years earlier. But the bus timing was bad and Elizabeth said she was able to go on. So, the toughest day of this tour continued. From Beauty Creek, the road climbs imperceptibly alongside the braided, gravel-banked, and milky Sunwapta River and then suddenly gets really steep. After an eternity on the unrelenting climb, the road goes past an overlook parking lot and over a false summit. I rode on ahead from there to tell the others they were coming. The downhill from the overlook and final climb to the chalet should have been easy. But, there was a stiff icy headwind flowing off the icefield and pouring downhill, making that last bit another energy-sucking challenge. When Dana and Elizabeth pulled up in front of the chalet steps, I ran out to give Elizabeth a celebratory hug. At Elizabeth's suggestion, they both got one. We truly appreciated dinner that evening, followed up by an easy 3 miles to the Hilda Creek Hostel still high up on the pass.

The rest of this trip was somewhat anticlimactic. We tried to get Gary and Marcy married by a Canadian Mountie at Honeymoon Lake but it didn't happen. John and Ruth were so strong and arrived so far ahead of us all that we began calling them the "Long Gones." The "Dave's Holiday" joke came from a Patty Larson song from the folk music festival about some "Dave" who goes to RV parks and sits in his lawn chair surrounded by plastic flamingos. Our "Dave's Holidays" were about the opposite of this. Elizabeth bought an Indian princess doll in Jasper and insisted on having the larger one. She knew it would be hers to carry back over Sunwapta and Bow Passes and then both ways over Kicking Horse Pass to and from Yoho. She got it anyway and then did just that. We saw hostel manager Tony again but this time at the Mosquito Creek Hostel. The Spray River buildings had been closed and removed, replaced by Banff's modern hostel building on Tunnel Mountain Road, Somehow, the heart and hearth aren't the same in this modern structure.

71

1995 - PATRICK RIDES AND ELIZABETH RETURNS

"Would you like to help us finish our dinner?" This was the third night in a row we asked this Japanese touring bicyclist the same question. We first encountered him struggling uphill with all his gear on his back near Rampart Creek Hostel, and thought he looked unprepared for the Rockies. He apparently expected meals to be available at the hostels. For three days he followed our itinerary and, luckily for him, we always prepared too much food. This was our 1995 Canadian Rockies trip, my sixth, and the one done by our one "child" out of five who hadn't yet done it, Dana's son Patrick, age 25. Elizabeth was back. She said, if Patrick went, she wanted to go again and, of course, with two of her children along, so was Dana, her third trip. Gary and Marcy repeated their ride of 1991, but without Gary's on-off-on behavior. Patrick hadn't trained much, or at all, but had been doing off-road riding and was strong. In any event, with his 15-year old "baby sister" along, complaining about the long miles, hard seat, big hills, etc., just wasn't an option.

We stayed in the new fancy Lake Louise Hostel. It had replaced the old Corral Creek Hostel and sauna where Gary had found Marcy four years earlier. I preferred the simpler hostel. The Lake Louise town site has changed drastically over the years and has come to resemble a modern suburban shopping mall with motels to rival Orlando. There was little more than a train stop, post office, and general store in the 70's. A positive discovery at lake Louise was Laggens bakery and deli. As usual, we took a group picture at the elevation sign at Sunwapta Pass. This time, Patrick climbed to the top of the sign for a dramatic view.

We were seeing a Backroads group on the road and met their young attractive leader, Sonia from Vancouver. Still-unmarried Patrick was especially good at meeting girls, biking and otherwise. This was a wet trip, and we waited out one rainstorm in a pine tree grove using our bike tarp as a makeshift shelter. We had our traditional hostel reunions with Tony at Mosquito Creek, Volker at Maligne Canyon, and Olga at Whiskey Jack. As far as we could recall, we knew all these from at least as far back as 1982.

We had a repeat of the unwanted peanut butter sandwich experience of 1973. This time it was leftover cold spaghetti and Patrick who had volunteered to carry it. We also discovered the Pub behind the

Saskatchewan River Crossing gift shop/cafeteria as the place of choice to eat, even to broiling our own steaks if desired.

In Field, B.C., we bought about $200 worth of food for the two days at Whiskey Jack Hostel up the Yoho Valley. We were about to distribute it to the group but still concerned that we would be able to carry it all. In addition, Dana's back was sore, and getting her up there was also a concern. We found help across the road where a bar was preparing for a big party. The two women there had to unload a truck full of beer. Our group made quick work of it in exchange for a lift for our half-ton of groceries, Dana and her bike. As we say back in Minnesota, it was a "heck of a deal."

The road to Wis key Jack.

2001 - DO YOU THINK THIS ONE'S A GRIZZLY?

"That's c-close enough Marv." Marv was stalking the bear with his camera and the bear kept glancing over his shoulder at him from about 25 feet away. We started planning how we were going to divide up Marv's stuff. His Canon, very good camera, wasn't included, unless one of us wanted to pry it out of the bear's mouth. We were on Kicking Horse Pass between Banff and Yoho Parks on the seventh *"Dave's Holiday"* Canadian Rockies bike tour (as nicknamed on the first NSSTC version of this ride in 1991). This was the fifth bear of this trip, one of them a grizzly for sure. We also saw elk, moose, goats, Rocky Mountain bighorn sheep, a pine martin, and a fox. We had the usual snowcapped mountains, interesting weather, good roads, friendly hostels, and a sometimes resemblance to the Tokyo subway at restaurants and gift shops. We were nine bicyclists, some on their first ever bike tour. All, except me as leader, were biking the Canadian Rockies for the first time. New this trip were a fearsome evening descent of Sunwapta Pass in the cold rain, a light vegetarian dinner for ravenous bikers after 77 miles that included two tough mountain passes, a rider afraid to do the downhills on her rented bike, and one tripper arriving 8 days late on a 12-day tour.

My trippers this time were Ed Rapoport, an old biking friend and NSSTC member from the early 70's, Tom O'Brien, my partner on the coast-to-coast ride of 1998 (and as our elder spokesman at 65 years, he sometimes called us his "sons"), Scott Weigle from Seattle whom Tom and I met in Montana 1998, Jim Nelson, a long-term Minneapolis biking friend, Marv Hondl Jim's coworker, and NS's Kitty Earl, Melissa Grannes, and Eva Schnasse (who arrived late).

"Where is Dave Siskind?" This question by Hostel Manager Olga at Whiskey Jack was the genesis for this, my seventh trip to the Canadian Rockies. I had prepared a bike trip itinerary for Cathy Marquardt, a NSSTC member, that she did with Jerry Youst in 1999. The Yoho Hostel manager, Olga, had been there since 1978 and remembered the previous visits by myself, family, and friends in 1982, 1986, 1991, and 1995. Cathy must have mentioned my name or that she was from Minnesota.

Of all my seven trips to the Canadian Rockies, this was the most complex to plan. Everyone had different ideas on how to get there. I also saw the chance to do something I've long wanted, biking to Banff from Glacier Park in Montana. I first simplified it for myself by specifying that the "official" trip starts in Banff. That let everyone make their own arrangements on how to get there and allowed me to make mine.

Ever since VIA, the Canadian National Railroad, discontinued Banff service, I have always wanted to avoid the long drive from Minneapolis by taking Amtrak to Glacier Park in Montana and riding up to Banff. Because wife Dana wasn't on this Canadian Rockies trip as she had been in 1986, 1991, and 1995, driving wasn't an attractive alternative. Also, on the first trip out there in 1973, we bypassed the Ribbon Creek Hostel in Kananaskis Country because the road to it was then unridable coarse gravel. This tour, July 2001, was a chance to do all these things. Tom and Scott were coming from the west coast by train and also liked the idea of biking up from Glacier Park. With Jim, flying out to Kalispell to bike Glacier Park's Going-to-the-Sun Highway, there would be four of for that ride north to Banff.

My part of this adventure started with the traditional seven-day bike ride to Winnipeg, Canada for the four-day folk music festival, a 13-year family tradition. After the festival and on her way home, by van, Dana dropped me and bike off in Fargo, North Dakota. From there, I could catch Amtrak to the west. (I did not realize I could have boarded a little closer, in Grand Forks). Having about eight hours to kill, I rode around Fargo and located the train station. I also found a nice bike path along the Red River that led to a park and campground where I talked them into letting me shower, for free. Still riding around, restless, I saw a feuding couple and reporting them to the police and then met North Carolina bicyclist Chuck Tharp. We waited in a convenience store booth till about midnight, snacking and people watching. It was great late-night people watching. Chuck was training to Havre, Montana and planning to bike from there through North Dakota back to Fargo. We boxed our bikes and waited till about 5 a.m. when the two hours late westbound Empire Builder arrived.

I did not sleep well on the train, but was awake enough to appreciate the warm greetings from Tom and Scott on the East Glacier train platform. They had arrived from Portland and Seattle on the eastbound Empire Builder that morning and had been hanging around waiting for me. As per Scott's recommendation, we had dinner in Buzz's Brew Station and then rode the 0.8 miles to Brownie's Bakery and Hostel. We met up with Jim the next day in Babb, north of St. Mary. The four of us were all flying pretty high.

Four of us rode north from East Glacier in Montana to Banff via St. Mary, Chief Mountain Highway, and Waterton Lakes National Park. We were starved when we arrived with 80 hilly miles (one downhill good for 48.3 mph) and after checking in at the hostel were immediately lured into the local pizza parlor for a double dose. We also set the pattern for the trip that first night, exploring the local area, looking for treats like milkshakes, and meeting other bike tourists in the nearby campground. A Dutch cycling couple were camping who had been on the road for 22 months. So much for impressing others with *our* exploits. We saw the trip's first bear on the final approach to Watertown and, as part of our departure the next day, explored the grand Prince of Wales Lodge on the hill.

Dramatic Glacier National Park mountains were in sight on our left all that first day. We continued on the east side of the Divide the next day through more prairie-like terrain as the mountains receded into the distance in the west. Passing through Pincer Creek, I replaced my reading glasses that I had sat on the day before, and admired the windmill farms on the neighboring hills. It was windy, luckily on our backs. We were heading for the dramatic Kananaskis Country and hoped the Alberta roadmap was accurate - that the road was paved all the way to the Trans-Canada Highway outside Banff.

Other bikers were coming towards us into the strong southern wind, heading for Crowsnest Pass to enter the Parks via the west side. They had started in Calgary. We had decided against doing Crowsnest for now so we could do it as part of our return south in three weeks, a good choice for us. We also encountered one of our own, Marv Hondl, driving his pickup around with his bike and Kitty's on top. He was to meet us in Banff in four days but knew about where we would be and decided to "look us up." I suspect he was tempted to ditch the truck and join us a wheel, but, practicality won out.

We camped in Chain Lakes Provincial Park, and were happy to find a food concession open in this relatively empty place. Tom tried his darndest to hint his way into a shower from a motorized camper man, to no avail. The next day, we ducked in out of a rainstorm and clouds of biting flies at the Highwood River Inn B&B on the Kananaskis Highway. While deciding if we wanted to stop for the day, we helped

76

the owner bring some window room dividers inside. It was a good stop - friendly, great food, *showers*, and with a basement movie theater. We set up tents to dry, I washed some clothes, and later had a nice, but one-way, conversation with my wife's answering machine. Staying there was about right for making Ribbon Creek Hostel the next day, 63 miles. The owner, Chris Thorburn, told us about his and his wife's experiences as cruise ship entertainers and also what we should expect the next day. We had not a clue about either of these things.

The next morning's ride was uphill a long way. In fact, we were going up the highest paved pass in Canada, to 7,239 ft (2,206 m), with its resident grizzly. The newly paved road was fine, the mountains were close and extremely rugged, much like those to the north in the national parks, and the grizzley was sufficiently far that neither he nor us felt threatened. Tom said the mountains seem to go on forever and around every bend there are more. Near Ribbon Creek, we explored the upscale shopping and eating area, the deserted ski area, and saw another bear which was of disputed type. The next day we made it to Banff and the rendezvous with the rest of our group except, as it turned out, for delayed Eva.

After the "official" 12-day Banff, etc. tour, the same group, but without Scott who left the trip in Jasper, returned to East Glacier via the other or west side of the Continental Divide: Kootenay Park, Radium Hot Springs, Skookumchuck, Fernie, Crowsnest Pass, Pincher Creek, and Cardston. At Crowsnest Pass I saw a mention of the Treadwell Mine. After pondering awhile (with CRS it usually takes awhile, if ever), I remembered a song by James Keeleghan about this mine. It's one of my favorite songs by one of my favorite singer-song writers, a Canadian from Alberta no less. Unfortunately there was no way I could adequately share this with my fellow travelers. It's one of those "you had to be there" things.

The central part of this experience and reason for all this riding around is the 12-day Banff-Jasper-Yoho tour. For this, we all met in Banff. Ed, Melissa, and Kitty flew out to Calgary. Marv drove out with a few tourist stops on the way including, as mentioned, running into the four of us biking near Kananaskis Country. Eva had the hardest time, driving out, breaking down near Valley City, North Dakota, and finally flying out to Calgary.

Even with the great and not so great, it was another fine adventure. After our wet, cold experience going over Sunwapta Pass going north, we had glorious sun and blue skies for the return the following week. The many days that first week with rain showers and low clouds in the mountain tops were replaced by mostly sunny days the second week, and the weather was cool rather than the torrid July conditions we heard about back in the Twin Cities. In total, only one day was really bad - a miserable 20 miles from Beauty Creek Hostel to Sunwapta Falls restaurant into a cold wind and rain. That morning tested our resolve as we shivered, looked through our panniers for dry clothes, and waited for it to quit while drying out around the restaurant's fireplace.

While there, we negotiated with the restaurant people for food to take along for that day's dinner. Kitty talked a ranger into giving her a lift to Jasper where she could find a warm and cozy hotel room. The rain stopped, enabling the rest of us to pleasantly bike to the warm and cozy Athabasca Hostel. The next worse rain was the morning we were to depart from Mosquito Creek Hostel heading for Yoho Park when we waited for it to quit. Other problems were solved or somehow solved themselves. The timid downhiller used the inter-hostel shuttle to avoid the big downhills although she had no problems with the uphills. For three days after the meal deemed too light for the energy expended, the guys cooked and made sure the fare was hearty. Our late rider, Eva, finally arrived and had a great although short time. As on previous Canadian Rockies trips, we biked the big climbs up to Mt. Edith Cavell, Maligne Lake, and the Yoho valley and hiked the Iceline trail in Yoho, plus trails at Johnston and Maligne canyons.

This year 2001 trip had two touring styles and they were along gender lines. Our two young women, Kitty Earl and Melissa Grannes, were riding for workouts and training and therefore raced on ahead. Kitty is a marathoner and racer and attributed her speed to not having a granny gear. She also was our occasional medical angel of mercy. Melissa is used to getting in two intense hours of training-type riding on her racing bike. She found her rented loaded-up touring bike heavy and awkward and was not comfortable and confident on it. It was ironic that, before the tour, there was concern about the pace we would riding and that it might be too fast. The young women, as it turned out, were not on a trip that matched their wants and expectations. I still hope they enjoyed the experience or will come to feel that way someday.

The older married-with-children men were the tourists, especially Tom, Jim, Marv, and me. We rode together, stopped at overlooks together, and took pictures of the scenery and each other together. We stopped to talk with other bike tourists and even with a hiker going from Calgary to Vancouver with a large trailer in tow. This was Marv Hondl's first ever bike tour. He had a great time and asked, while still during this tour, when we could do another. Some of the guys, me included, thought Marv was our best cook. He and I were the most persistent photographers shooting everything except our young female bikers who were generally far ahead and out of sight. I hoped Marv's slides could be a future North Star Club meeting program.

Our third woman rider, Eva Schnasse, finally arrived via the airlines and shuttle from Calgary with tales of her adventures with citizens of Valley City, North Dakota, who had befriended her when her car broke down there. She later said the four days she had with us were a wonderful introduction to bike touring in a beautiful place. She stayed a few days extra at Lake Louise on her own. It made some of us tired just seeing how hard she worked on her bike. We became nuisances by harping on her to get off of her 52-tooth chainring and spin more. She tired of this and finally said to me "I'm not listening to you." That reminded me of home.

Stats: For those of us on the long tour, It was five days northbound (349 miles) and six south (453 miles). The "official" tour of Banff, Jasper, and Yoho Parks was 550 miles in 12 days, all in hostels with 30 meals for a very inexpensive $240 US, exclusive of transportation to and from Banff.

Bike troubles were minimal. Ed had worn-out tires and a loosening freewheel; Marv had one puncture on his racing-type tires; Kitty had a broken shift cable which the guys fixed, sorta; and I had some minor problems like a cracked pedal (it held till the end) and sometimes shaky bike (from a loose headset). One highlight was again seeing Olga Forbes, who still manages the Whiskey Jack hostel in Yoho. At 82 years of age, she remembers the previous Minnesota groups' visits. She said we shouldn't wait another six years if we want to see her again. Dana had some regrets about missing this trip and not getting to see Olga. I also missed seeing Tony Chatham, who we knew from previous trips at least back to 1982 at Mosquito Creek Hostel and before that at Spray River in Banff. He took the year off, and Olga wonders if he will return at all.

ANOTHER PERSPECTIVE ON THE 2001 TOUR - JIM'S

Tripper Jim Nelson is a long-term biking friend from the 1970's era Lake Country Cyclists. We've done hundreds of day rides together but only a few weekend tours, and one long ride - to the LAW Rally in Madison, Wisconsin in 1985. Even with a lot of serious riding experience, including Adventure Cycling's TransAm trail, the west coast, and Alaska, Jim, our normally reserved Norwegian, was really impressed with the Canadian Rockies. He e-mailed highlights to friends after this tour and a selection of them well sums up the adventure:

> "Hello from Minneapolis, my last note was from the Raging Elk Hostel in Fernie, Canada so I thought I'd do one more last note to let some of you know I survived the trip. It was an incredible trip, words do not begin to describe it, and my pictures do not come close to capturing the majesty, the beauty and the splendor of the mountains. Some Trip highlights for me were:

> Riding the Glacier Park "Going to the Sun" road and climbing over Logan Pass. It took just over three hours to make the climb, and I was in a 29-inch gear the entire way.

> Meeting Tom and Scott. I had read all about them in Dave's book. [Author: this is Bicycling the Adventure Cycling Northern Tier Trail Across America.]

> Riding on the Chief Mountain road with two big screaming downhill runs.

> Marv finding us on the Cowboy Trail road, out in the middle of nowhere, near Old Man River (Alberta) on Highway 22. He was in his pickup truck headed north.

> Finding a food stand open and run by friendly ladies at Chain Lakes Provincial Park [Author: this was in Alberta, in the middle of nowhere.]

> Seeing the incredible views at a picnic lunch alongside the road near the top of Highwood Pass We got the tuna can open (without a can opener) and had some of the best tuna sandwiches ever.

Trying to eat our way through the biggest, heaviest box of raisin bran cereal ever. I petered out at four bowls. Dave, Tom and Scott had at least two to three bowls each [Author: it was three] and the box was still at least 1/2 full. [Author: we left it behind]

Riding the gondola to the top of Sulfur Mountain at Banff.

On a cold, wet, overcast, rainy day, watching the clouds pour over the mountain tops like a gigantic, awesome, slow-motion waterfall. And then watching the clouds evaporate as they got to a lower elevation.

Witnessing Tom's uncanny ability to find coins and coin-like objects. He was able to find Kitty's brake lever dust cap (it was about the size of a nickel) in the bushes where it had been tossed.

Finding out my waterproof shoe covers worked superbly in the rain and cold, and were the envy of the others.

Watching the group go into a late night "feeding frenzy" at Athabasca Falls Hostel. The earlier lasagna dinner had not been big enough.

Cleaning up the mess after Marv and Ed made tacos at the Maligne Canyon Hostel. I think they used every pot, pan, dish and bowl in the place.

Looking down at the 30-meter waterfall in Maligne Canyon, right under the footbridge we were standing on.

Seeing the mysterious Medicine Lake. It has no overland outlet and was big medicine to the native Americans.

Seeing and hearing an avalanche come down off the Angel Glacier on Mt. Edith Cavell.

Finding little corkscrews of metal hanging off my bike's brake pads after coming down from Mt. Edith Cavell. It was metal scraped off my wheel rims after the long, wet, gritty downhill.

Hearing about Herman's carefree summer vacation adventures. [Author: a Dutchman bicyclist we met at several hostels.]

Seeing the sun set over the mountains and reflect in the water at the Beauty Creek Hostel.

Climbing up one side and screaming down the other side of Sunwapta Pass in the warm morning sun, one of the most incredible, indescribable, and beautiful biking experiences I've ever had.

Scrambling over the Athabasca glacier and jumping over the crevasses.

Watching Dave accidentally drop his hamburger in the cook fire and then try to salvage the pieces to make a sandwich.

Taking a hot sauna at Mosquito Creek Hostel and then jumping into the ice-cold crrrreeeek - twice! Marv and I must have woken everyone in the surrounding area with our yelling.

Not having to carry two-day's worth of food up to the Whiskey Jack Hostel. Melissa found someone to haul it up the hill for us in their van.

Standing in the spray and looking up at the huge 250- meter-high Takakkaw Falls in Yoho Park. The water dancing on the rocks mesmerized me.

Hiking the Ice Line Trail and looking down at the now tiny Takakkaw Falls.

Finding out Marv didn't snore at night, he "snorkeled."

Watching Marv on foot try to get closer to a bear, for a picture, while the bear leered suspiciously at him.

Riding down the 8% grade at Sinclair Pass and screaming into Radium Hot Springs. Hats off to Marv - he rode up and down each side of this big pass in one day.

Grinding it out against a big headwind to get to Skookumchuck for the night and finding a nice little log cabin hostel to stay in. A family of baby rabbits lived under it and came out to play on the lawn at dusk.

Riding on Highway 507 into Pincher Creek, another incredible, indescribable and beautiful biking experience for me. There were large rolling hills with deep green and bright yellow fields all around, blue sky with big white fluffy clouds overhead and the blue mountains in the background. We rode by an old one-room country schoolhouse and I thought of the country school I went to.

Running into Ron Erickson, MnDOT State Geometric Engineer, at a cafe in Pincher Creek, Alberta. [Author: It's a small world, Ron works in the same office as Jim]

Being detoured from Kiowa to Browning because of a forest fire. We had a big tailwind that blew us 12 miles down the hill to Browning in a few minutes, and had a long gruesome headwind uphill 12 miles to get back to East Glacier to end the trip.

Having a few "Moose Drool" brown ales at East Glacier to celebrate the end of an incredible trip".

AND YET ANOTHER PERSPECTIVE - TOM'S

Tom also wrote up his thoughts on the trip. Some of his highlights were similar to Jim's:

"The snow-capped mountains just jump up from the valleys. There are lakes and streams everywhere. Wild life is all around you. We climbed many hills and crossed the Continental Divide four times. We had rain, clouds, blue skies, cold, sun and heat."

Like Jim, Tom had a "small-world" experience that he describes:

"July 9. I loaded up my bike and rode to the Portland Amtrak Station (16 miles). As I pulled up to the station I saw two other bikers who had just got off the train and were ready to head to Astoria (Oregon). I found out that they were planning on riding across the USA. When I told them that I was heading for East Glacier to meet some others and then head north into the Canadian Rockies, they said, "You're Tom and you are wearing your blue shirt." Who were these two riders and how did they know me?"

"Well, let me tell you just how small this world is. In 1999, David (my friend who rode coast-to-coast with me in 1998) rode from his home, in Minneapolis, to Oregon so that we could ride Cycle Oregon together. On this ride he met a lady (Mary) who lives in Madison, Wisconsin, and they have stayed in contact. About four months ago David rode to Madison to see Mary. During this visit Mary introduced David to her friend and his son who were thinking about riding cross country this year. Yes, these were Mary's friends. They knew me from reading David's book about our cross-country trip in 1998. If I had not been five hours early for my train I would have never met them. After some more talk they headed for their adventure, and I packed my bike in one of their train boxes and sat down to wait for the train to leave for my adventure."

Tom's thoughts on the Kananaskis Country Highwood River Inn B&B:

"The owners had spent many years as entertainers on cruise ships with a magic and dance act. What I found ironic is that while we were staying in this most wonderful place, the owner's wife and daughter were off camping for the night with some friends."

Tom wrote this the day after we crossed Highwood Pass and biked to Ribbon Creek Hostel near the Kananaskis Village Resort:

"The resort was full of shops and fine restaurants. We selected a pub, sort of out of the way from the main crowd, and went in. The host took one look at us and asked if we were looking for something more *upscale*. I wonder what he saw!! Here we were, just finished riding 72 miles over the highest road in Canada, unshowered, still in bike clothes (as if we had anything else to wear), and with helmet hair. We answered that his place would do. Dinner was outside on the deck with a great view all around. I had fish and chips."

"After dinner, we decided to take a ride up the hill to the Nakiska Ski Area which was specifically designed to host the alpine events of the 1988 Calgary Winter Olympics. By the way, the place is for sale. On the way to the ski area, we saw our first up-close bear. There was some debate as to if it was a grizzly or a black bear. I voted for grizzly."

Tom's experience at the Sunwapta Falls restaurant after our cold, rainy 20-mile ride:

"When I finally reached our lunch stop, Sunwapta Falls, the others were having their lunch. I walked right pass them and straight to the souvenir part of this complex. The lady asked if she could help me and I said, "yes." "I would like another layer," I told her, and it must be waterproof. She brought out a coat that said it was waterproof and I said "sold." No, I did not ask the price. After all, what good is money if I freeze to death? The jacket, actually a parka, is made of waterproof and breathable microfiber with a zip-out Sherpa fleece liner. When I went to sign the Visa slip I could not get my hand to write my name. Did I say I was COLD? I put on the jacket and returned to the restaurant where my new jacket was affectionately named THE BIG COAT. I was now warm and stayed warm for the rest of the tour. The rain had stopped by now. I think it was afraid of THE BIG COAT." [Author: It really was a nice coat and at a reasonable price. I could have used a new one myself but didn't want to carry it.]

The Mount Edith Cavell Hostel is about a kilometer from the end of the road where begins the Cavell Glacier interpretive trail. Tom wrote about this place:

"With the rain coming to a halt I headed to the road's end to get a better look at the mountain and the glacier. You guessed it, it started to rain again so I headed back to the Hostel. The views of the towering mountain that surround the Hostel were outstanding. What a place. I could have stayed there for a week just looking at the surrounding mountains. Some of our group hiked up to the base of the glacier. They saw several avalanches high up on the mountain."

"The 11,031-foot peak of Mt. Edith Cavell towers over every mountain in the Jasper National Park. In a cirque valley on the northeast slope of the mountain is the famous Angel Glacier, suspended as if in full flight with it's huge icy wings outstretched. In a narrow valley below is our hostel. The brilliant colors of the Cavell Meadows and the turquoise waters of the lake below are only a few of the wonderful sites."

For the day we left Skoocumchuck and rode to Fernie, Tom wrote:

"By going north we began the slow and steady climb towards Crowsnest Pass and rode upstream along the Elk River. It was a very beautiful ride through the canyon. When I reached Fernie I realized that this was no small town, population 4,900. Our overnight would be at The Raging Elk Hostel. If you ever visit Fernie and stay at the Raging Elk, you will find they have a 5 day activity plan all laid out for you".

"As for us, the only plan was a hot shower, dinner, and some ice cream. As a special surprise, we found that our room had its own shower. We did a quick tour of the town and located a restaurant and the ice cream shop. The ice cream was a very good deal, with the cost being only $1.00 (about $0.66 US) for a scoop. It was a good size scoop at that. Another great day."

"About the Raging Elk Hostel: A couple took over the Sundowner Motel and Hostel and revamped it into the Raging Elk Hostel, a year round adventure base camp for travelers and adventurers alike. This hostel looks, on the outside, like a huge warehouse. Inside it's a maze of rooms (mostly public rooms and not the rooms that you sleep in), which are painted with a wide selection of colors and designs. There is a very large kitchen and a TV/video room with a dozen couches of various designs and colors to sit on. It's a very interesting place."

Like Jim and the author, Tom also liked the back road to Pincher Creek. He recalled one amusing incident:

"Highway 3 is a major route for cars and trucks. It has a pretty good shoulder and is mostly flat. As we rode along David talked about taking a secondary road that another cyclist had suggested. David said that this secondary road should be quiet and peaceful. We made a right turn onto Highway 507. David in front and Jim and I just behind. At that moment, a Corvette also made a screaming right turn and the driver put the pedal to the metal. The Vette went flying by David. Jim and I broke out into laugher - so much for this quiet and peaceful road. About three miles down this road we passed the Corvette, which was parked on the side with the hood up. After the Vette experience, the road turned very nice. Yes, there were more hills than on the main highway but it was worth it. This is farm land and very beautiful."

RETROSPECT ON THESE TRIPS

The Canadian Rocky Mountain Parks are still beautiful and dramatic but, like everything else in western society, have changed over the years. One major addition is the Japanese tourists. The signs in the store windows show that Banff is bilingual: English and Japanese. Scott commented on the restaurants and gift shops resembling the Tokyo subway when caravans of tour buses arrived. The morning rides toward the Columbia Icefield are accompanied by a frantic and constant northern flow of these buses, cars, and recreational vehicles. Fortunately, the road has a wide paved shoulder, or the bicycling would be less than fun, even dangerous. In the afternoon there is a reverse flow. Traffic is considerably less north of Sunwapta Pass and the Icefield because Jasper is smaller and less visited than the Banff and Lake Louise areas. Except for local deliveries, trucks are banned on the Icefields Parkway, and the traffic all but disappears in the still-light evening hours. Some years we saw road repairs that would still be going on during the next visit, four or five years later.

One big recent change was the absence of elk on the streets and lawns in the Banff and Jasper townsites. The elk were apparently relocated away from the populated areas and are reported not to be doing well. Also noticed near the towns are fences along the roads to keep wildlife off the busy traveled portions, especially the Trans-Canada Highway.

A very minor change, although significant for us, was the absence of the elevation signs at the passes, particularly Sunwapta. The Sunwapta sign was a traditional milestone and where we always took a group photo.

The "bike touring" season in the northern Rockies is basically July and August, but even in that narrow window, it can still be cold and even snow, especially at high elevations. The Yoho Valley is generally inaccessible until early July. September can be nice, although snow risks are higher. Hotels, cabin camps, and campgrounds are options. My preference in these parks is the chain of close-spaced hostels. They are cozy and neat, great places to meet other travelers, and for the most part, are bear-free. They are also inexpensive, have cooking facilities, and some have food service or food to sell. Backroads and similar organized tours mostly seem to camp, in preference to the hostels, except the NYC 43rd Street Y, which had been doing Canadian Rockies trips for decades, although they were not evident recently.

I have bicycled other mountains in 40 years of biking: the Appalachians from North Carolina to New Hampshire, Snowden in northern Wales, the Alps in France, Switzerland and Austria, the Dolomites in Italy, the Fjords of Norway, and the Dinaric Alps in Yugoslavia. But, it is the Canadian Rockies I think of, perhaps too egotistically, as "my mountains." It is in those Canadian National Parks that I have shared so much awe and wonder with friends and family. Even the Going-to-the Sun Highway in Glacier Park was grand to me mostly because it resembled the Canadian Rockies. My fantasy is about living in Banff. As my wife would say if I told her that: "In your dreams."

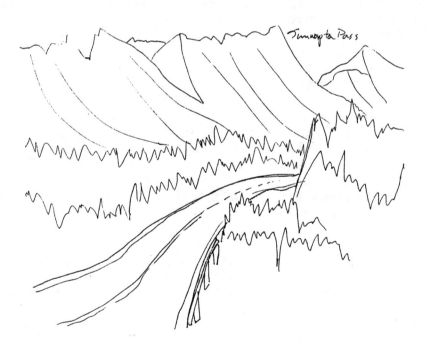